22 50 Apple

22.50

JUNIOR ROOM

MODERN
NATIONS
—OF THE—
WORLD

SOUTH KOREA

MODERN
NATIONS
—OF THE—
WORLD

SOUTH KOREA

BY JEAN K. WILLIAMS

LUCENT BOOKS
P.O. BOX 289011
SAN DIEGO, CA 92198-9011

Library of Congress Cataloging-in-Publication Data

Williams, Jean K., 1957–
    South Korea / by Jean K. Williams.
        p.   cm. — (Modern nations of the world)
    Includes bibliographical references and index.
    Summary: Discusses the history, geography, culture, and current
state of South Korea, a land of both tradition and modern development.
    ISBN 1-56006-446-3 (lib. bdg. : alk. paper)
    1. Korea (South)—Juvenile literature.   2. Korea—History—
Juvenile literature.   [1. Korea (South)]   I. Title. II. Series.
    DS907.4.W55   1999
    951.95—DC21
                                                            98-34605
                                                            CIP
                                                            AC

Copyright © 1999 by Lucent Books, Inc.
P.O. Box 289011, San Diego, CA 92198-9011
Printed in the U.S.A.

CONTENTS

INTRODUCTION
SOUTH KOREA: FROM HERMIT KINGDOM TO WORLD STAGE

In the Far East is a fascinating land known to few Westerners until the twentieth century. Yet in the histories of its larger neighbors, China, Japan, and Russia, the nation of Korea has played a significant part. Not quite large or powerful enough to control its own destiny in modern times, Korea has always been attractive enough, rich in natural and human resources, to be of much interest to its neighbors.

Korea can boast of many cultural triumphs. The major world religion of Buddhism flourished there, inspiring magnificent temples and religious art during Europe's Dark Ages. The concept of movable type was put to use in Korea well before it revolutionized Western culture in the fifteenth century. In more recent years the Korean capital city of Seoul has been at the center of a remarkable transformation: One of the poorest countries in the world, ravaged by civil war, emerged within a few short decades as a wealthy, increasingly active participant in international affairs.

But Korea has also gone through many difficult experiences in the twentieth century. Its enduring tragedy, the division of its traditional territory into two parts, sparked a destructive civil war in the 1950s. There was no victor in the Korean War, which ended in a stalemate, and the peninsula on which the ancient country was formed remains divided today. This division is enforced by the so-called Demilitarized Zone (DMZ), a fearsome combination of armed troops and land mines in a 2.5-mile-wide strip of land stretching across the peninsula.

Why was the six hundred-mile-long Korean peninsula, a united country for more than thirteen hundred years, split in two? Like many other decisions with ultimately undesirable effects, it had seemed a good idea at the time.

For most of the first half of the twentieth century, Korea was under the control of its powerful eastern neighbor, Japan. Therefore, when World War II ended with the defeat

KOREA

of Japan in 1945, there was no native Korean government, elected or otherwise, to take charge. Thus troops of two of the victorious nations, the United States and the Union of Soviet Socialist Republics (USSR), occupied the peninsula to ensure the orderly departure of the Japanese and to provide stability in the early days of what was supposed to have been Korean independence.

The United States did in fact help the south establish an independent government. But the Soviet Union, seeking to realize a centuries-old dream of controlling access to a warm-water port, refused to withdraw according to plans drawn up near the end of the war. That is why the 38th parallel, or line of latitude, which divided the U.S. zone from the Soviet zone, became, in 1948, the official dividing line between two new countries: the Republic of Korea in the south and the Democratic People's Republic of Korea in the north.

South Korea, as the Republic of Korea is also called, has a vibrant society that embraces much of modern life while cherishing many elements of its traditional culture. The people work hard: South Korea has one of the longest work-weeks in the world, and high school students think nothing of a sixteen-hour day of classes and studying. Those qualities helped transform South Korea from a poor, rural economy in the 1960s to a major exporter of manufactured goods in two decades. By the 1980s, Korean products were everywhere, and its people had moved from cottages in farming villages to high-rise apartment buildings in bustling cities.

But in spite of the modern trappings, South Korea remains a land of tradition. *Hanbok*, the colorful traditional clothing, is worn on special holidays. Ceremonies that show reverence for ancestors and family elders is evidence of a Confucian heritage. Koreans are a people of contrasts: loyal employees accustomed to a strong tradition of authority, yet fiercely competitive in school, in sports, and in business. Moreover, Korean university students have never been shy about

Korean women dressed in costume play traditional instruments. South Koreans incorporate their rich cultural heritage into modern society.

protesting government wrongs. It is thanks to that tradition of protest that South Korea has moved from being a democracy in name only to the ideal of a true republic with regular, free elections.

Korea is also a land of much beauty, surrounded on three sides by the sea. Snow covers the mountaintops in winter, and vacationers gather at the beaches in the hot, muggy summers. The ancient name of Korea was Choson, translated as "Land of the Morning Calm." Though their history has experienced few periods of calmness, the people of South Korea are optimistic about one day reuniting, peacefully, with their northern brethren.

1

SOUTH KOREA: THE LAND

> Alone, cup in hand,
> I view the distant peaks. . . .
> The peaks neither speak nor smile;
> But what happiness! O what joy!
> —from the poem *New Songs in the Mountain*
> by fifteenth-century Korean Yun Son-do

To enjoy a view of distant peaks in Korea, one must simply live there—anywhere. Mist-covered peaks are visible from any point in South Korea, a small country carved from an ancient land in 1948.

THE "HERMIT KINGDOM" OF ASIA

South Korea and the more than three thousand islands it comprises make up about 45 percent of what was once Korea. South Korea's 45.5 million people squeeze into about the same amount of land as the state of Virginia, or about 38,370 square miles, one of the highest population densities in the world. Though for several hundred years Korean people called their country Choson, Europeans referred to it as Korea, a name derived from the medieval-era Koryo dynasty (935–1392). The "Hermit Kingdom" was another name for Korea, which tried as much as possible to keep to itself and maintain independence from its more powerful neighbors.

Korea is strategically located between China to its west across the Yellow Sea, Manchuria (today part of China) and a sliver of Siberian Russia to the north, and the islands that make up Japan to the east. Thus it has often served as both a bridge or stopover point between the various Eastern superpowers and their armies and a conductor of culture from points west, such as China and India, to Japan. Across the East Sea, or Sea of Japan, the South Korean city of Pusan is only about fifty miles from the Japanese islands of Kyushu and Honshu.

On a map, the outline of the Korean peninsula looks like a rabbit, with its ears attached to the Chinese mainland and its curving back lapped by the Sea of Japan. A volcanic outgrowth formed the peninsula more than 2 billion years ago,

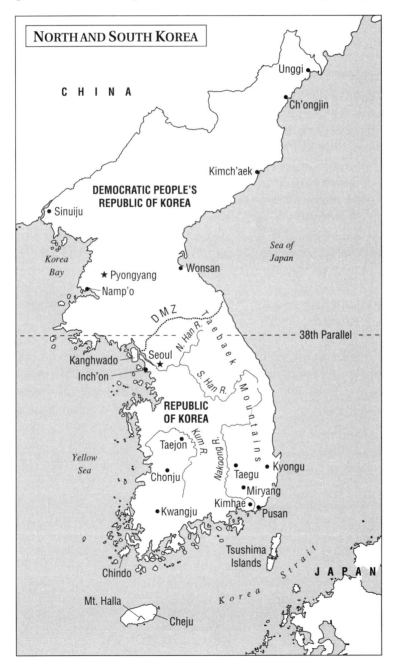

NORTH AND SOUTH KOREA

CHINA

Unggi

Ch'ongjin

Kimch'aek

DEMOCRATIC PEOPLE'S
REPUBLIC OF KOREA

Sinuiju

Korea
Bay

Sea of
Japan

★ Pyongyang

Wonsan

Namp'o

D M Z

N. Han R.

T
a
e
b
a
e
k

38th Parallel

Kanghwado

Seoul
★

Inch'on

S. Han R.

M
o
u
n
t
a
i
n
s

REPUBLIC
OF KOREA

Yellow
Sea

Taejon

Kum R.

Nakdong R.

Chonju

Kyongu

Taegu

Miryang

Kimhae

Kwangju

Pusan

Tsushima
Islands

S
t
r
a
i
t

J A P A N

Chindo

K o r e a

Mt. Halla

Cheju

making it half as old as the earth itself. Natural mineral resources are fairly scarce in South Korea, but it does contain
about half of the farmable land of the peninsula. Korea is just
west of the Pacific Ocean's "ring of fire," an area of much volcanic activity. Though there has been no active volcano on
the Korean peninsula for more than nine hundred years,
there are occasional mild earthquake tremors.

A MOUNTAINOUS TOPOGRAPHY

Glaciers did not move far enough south to smooth out the
peninsula, so South Korea remains a rugged piece of land,
70 percent covered by mountains, earning it the nickname
"Switzerland of Asia," even though most of South Korea's
mountains are of relatively low elevation. Hallasan, or Mount
Halla, is South Korea's highest peak. A volcanic peak south
of the peninsula on Chejudo, the island of Cheju, it climbs
to an elevation of sixty-four hundred feet. The Taebaek, or
"Great White," Mountains are South Korea's biggest mountain range and form a line paralleling the eastern coast of
the peninsula.

Although most of Korea's land is mountainous, some flat
lowlands are suitable for farming. Most of these are in west
Korea's coastal plains where rivers such as the Han and the
Kum fan out before emptying into the Yellow Sea, providing
the plains with rich, alluvial soil. All lowlands are divided by
mountains or at least hills, and even the largest sections are
only 150 to 160 square miles in size. In the mountainous
eastern part of South Korea, farmland is much more scarce
and narrow. Rice is the country's staple food, though poor

HOT SPRINGS

While Korea lies beyond the Pacific rim hub of
volcanic activity, there is enough thermal activity below the
country's surface to generate hot springs. Their water temperature ranges from approximately 120°F to 170°F. Some, like
those at Pugok and Suanbo, are of historical interest. There are
many mineral springs, too, which people believe to have cura-
tive powers for ailments such as rheumatism or eczema. But
some Koreans just like to drink the mineral water, considering
it an all-around health benefit.

Mount Halla, a volcanic mountain on Chejudo, is the highest peak in South Korea.

harvests in recent years have forced the country to import rice to meet demand. Other major crops are legumes, barley, and vegetables.

RUGGED COASTS, THOUSANDS OF ISLANDS

The western and southern coasts of the Korean peninsula are vastly different from the east coast. Higher in elevation, the eastern shoreline is quite smooth with barely an indentation, while the west and south coasts are full of little peninsulas and bays. Many bays along the western shore are quite shallow, and in recent years, much land has been reclaimed from the sea by filling in the bays with soil, making these areas usable for agriculture. That trend is expected to continue. Because of its shallowness, the western coastal area is also prone to saltwater flooding at high tides.

The tides along the western shore can vary greatly, especially at the port of Inch'on; the only place in the world with a greater tidal variation is Canada's Bay of Fundy. The western coast provides Koreans with a bounty of clams, oysters, shrimp, snails, and abalone. A variety of waterbirds, like the fabulous Manchurian crane, are attracted to the easy fishing to be had in the coast's shallow inlets and coves. The crane was almost extinct less than thirty years ago, and is still an endangered species.

The Yellow, or West, Sea is quite shallow, in general, its depth is usually less than 325 feet, and so it cannot accommodate the large shipping vessels that go in and out of eastern and southern ports. The Yellow Sea earned its name because its water is tinted yellow-brown by soil washed down from China's Yangtze and Huangho Rivers.

Along the south and southeast shore of Korea is the Korea Strait, a thirty-four-mile-wide waterway between Korea and Japan that connects the Yellow Sea and East Sea. Like the western shoreline, Korea's southern coast is jagged, dotted with islands, and has many natural harbors, whose blue-green waters are deep enough to allow for large ships as well as deep sea fishing. The busiest harbor is at Pusan, which looks directly across the Korea Strait to the Japanese Tsushima Islands. The southern coast is the country's most picturesque and the center of Korea's seaweed and oyster farming.

The mountains of east Korea slope down to the East Sea, and the land continues its steep descent under the cold, deep blue water. The water's depth is great enough to accommodate large ocean vessels, and since there are few natural harbors along the smooth east coast, ports have been created there. Because it also contains a meeting point of warm and cold currents, making it attractive to an abundant fish and sea animal population, the East Sea is ideal for deep-sea fishing. Although the seas closer to North Korea can freeze, the Japanese current warms the East Sea waters, and it seldom freezes.

Thousands of islands are scattered just off South Korea's western and southern coasts. Most of them are uninhabited,

Chejudo is the largest island in South Korea and is inhabited by half a million people. Locals and tourists alike are attracted to the island's temperate weather and beautiful beaches.

THE ISLAND "OVER THERE"

If Korea was once the "Hermit Kingdom," then Chejudo was perhaps one of the shyest parts of that kingdom. *Cheju* means "over there," and *do* means "island." Located off the southwest tip of the Korean peninsula, "the Island Over There" is largest among South Korea's three thousand islands. After centuries of relative obscurity, the island has finally caught the attention of world travelers.

Its climate is among the most temperate in Korea, and its volcanic beaches and rock formations have led some to call it the "Hawaii of the Orient," although winter can, and does, pay visits there. The first tourists to arrive in the 1950s found a quaint and beautiful island whose inhabitants spoke a unique dialect and sometimes wore the same fashions, such as fur hats or stockings, introduced by Mongolian conquerors in the thirteenth century. The Mongols introduced horse breeding to the island, and ponies still run wild on the island. And there is a tradition on Chejudo of women divers who stay underwater for several minutes at a time.

Today, the island boasts hotels, golf courses, and paved roads as more travelers seek out its rugged beauty and free-roaming horses.

with two major exceptions being the picturesque Chejudo to the south and Kanghwado just south of the Demilitarized Zone. Chejudo is South Korea's largest island, and more than a half-million people live there. These and other islands belonging to South Korea are the tips of volcanic mountains, and were once peninsulas.

SHALLOW RIVER WATERS REQUIRE SPECIAL BOATS

South Korea's rivers are shallow and broad, navigable most of the year only by boats crafted especially for shallow waters. Even so, portions of many of the rivers may be too shallow for any kind of marine traffic. River depths can vary greatly, because about half of the country's yearly rainfall comes during two summer months. Floods often occur then, due not only to heavy rainfall but also to soil washed down from higher elevations, where the rivers originate, and which then settles onto the river bottoms, making the riverbeds even more shallow. In recent years more dams have been built or levees raised to control flooding and generate electricity. In drier seasons, smaller river- or streambeds might be completely dry.

South Korea's Han River, which springs from the west slopes of the Taebaek Mountains, is that country's most significant waterway that empties into the Yellow Sea. Seoul was

Riverboats, such as this pleasure boat on the Han River, are specially designed to travel South Korea's wide, shallow rivers.

settled alongside the Han, which is the country's second-longest river, looping through mid–South Korea before it turns north and empties at the western end of the Demilitarized Zone. The Nakdong in the southern part of South Korea is the country's longest, flowing from the Taebaek Mountains into the Korea Strait at the city of Pusan. South Korea's eastern rivers generally originate in the mountains and flow west, with no significant rivers emptying into the East Sea.

On South Korea's Mount Halla is a natural crater lake, and other lakes are human-made reservoirs. Although a few reservoirs were created hundreds of years ago, most were built since the Korean War, and one of them is more than forty miles long.

CLIMATE OF FOUR SEASONS

South Korea has four distinct seasons, which is typical at its Northern Hemisphere latitude. South Korea is about as far north of the equator as southern Spain, Kashmir, northern California, or the Middle Atlantic states. The southern part of the country is warmer than the north, and the island of Cheju has the balmiest winter weather. Not surprisingly, the highest mountainous areas tend to be the coldest in winter, especially in the interior of the peninsula.

Whereas winters in the northern part of the peninsula are bitterly cold, the monsoon winds traveling over the oceans and carrying hot, humid air in the summers tend to warm the southernmost part of the country. The east coast is usually slightly warmer in the winter than the west, because the Taebaek Mountains shelter it from the frigid air that can blow down from Manchuria or Siberia.

Summers in South Korea are hot, humid, and wet, especially in July and August, when much of the year's forty inches of rain falls. The monsoon season begins in June, but the winds pick up their full force in July, when hot weather and rain arrive and stay. By then the beaches are packed with tourists anxious to flee the hotter and more humid cities in the central part of the country—Seoul temperatures can reach a very muggy 100°F during the summer.

With much of the year's rainfall occurring in such a short time, flooding is likely to strike somewhere in South Korea each monsoon season; many dams have been built in recent decades to prevent that situation. The winds shift again in September, bringing clear skies along with cooler, dryer temperatures; most crops are harvested then. October is generally dry, breezy, and sunny. The trees on the mountains turn their rainbow of hues against bright blue skies.

In December, winter arrives. There is plenty of cold weather—temperatures in Seoul can drop into single digits—but winter remains relatively dry, although the farther north one goes on the peninsula, the more snow can be seen. Like autumn, spring brings delightful relief from extreme temperatures, and cherry trees and shrubs like azalea are in full bloom.

The scenic crater lake on Mount Halla is one of the few natural lakes in South Korea.

The rose of Sharon endured Japanese efforts to wipe out the long-standing symbol of Korean culture and is now the national flower of South Korea.

KOREANS SAVED THE ROSE OF SHARON, BUT THE TIGER IS GONE

Korea's foliage is much like that in China or Japan. Buddhist monks created beautiful temple gardens where native plants, such as the gingko tree, are showcased. Korea's forests and woodlands are covered with spring-blooming azaleas, and some shrubs such as holly, box-wood, and viburnums are abundant enough to be regarded as weeds. The wildflower cosmos lines roadsides, and a variety of trees are planted along city streets. The national flower of South Korea is the rose of Sharon, which is actually a shrub with a pink or purple trumpetlike flower. In some parts of Korea that flowering shrub was almost stamped out during the Japanese occupation, but Korean citizens unceasingly resisted efforts to exterminate their culture and language, and the rose of Sharon was secretly cultivated.

The southern part of South Korea is warm enough for orange and tangerine groves, and farther north are apple, pear, persimmon, and peach trees. Other common trees in South Korea include the maple, elm, willow, birch, oak, poplar, and pine, as well as nut trees such as walnut, chest-nut, and the gingko.

The traditional symbol of Korea was a species of Siberian tiger that once roamed the mountainous areas but is now ex-tinct. Korea's other large wildlife, such as black or brown bears, water deer, wolves, or wildcats, can still be found in the mountains and lowlands.

The peninsula is a stopover point for migratory birds such as crows, herons, cranes, sparrows, robins, and quails, flying to winter grounds in Southeast Asia or Australia. It also is on the migratory route of geese, ducks, swans, and white egrets. Occasionally, a lucky bird-watcher catches a glimpse of the rare Steller's sea eagle or white-tailed sea eagle.

SEOUL: BURSTING WITH PEOPLE, HISTORY, AND CULTURE

As beautiful as the Korean countryside is, most South Koreans live in cities, and the biggest city by far is the capital, Seoul, which reflects the ancient tradition as well as the ambitious future of its people. Of the old city gates that once connected the ten-mile wall surrounding the city, five remain and are proudly maintained and preserved, and the especially impressive South Gate has been incorporated into the city's main thoroughfare. The palaces and royal gardens of long-ago royal families are still open to visitors, but just beyond them lie modern commuter train and highway systems. Square mile upon square mile (102 in all) are filled with high-rise apartment buildings, office towers, and bustling factories. More than eighty colleges and universities are there, and Seoul is home to more than 10 million people, making it the fourth-largest city in the world after Tokyo, Shanghai, and Mexico City. About one-fourth of South Korea's population are residents of Seoul.

Settled along the Han River in a basin between the Bukhan Mountains and Nam Mountain and thirty-seven miles inland from the Yellow Sea, the city of Hansong first served as a capital in 1393. Its newer name, Seoul, was adopted at the end of World War II and means "the capital" in the Korean language.

The Korean War years were devastating to Seoul, which was the target of constant bombings by North Korea. At one point Seoul's population dropped to fifty thousand people. After the war ended the Republic of Korea instituted an ambitious recovery program, and succeeded at a rapid pace. Traditionally a rural country, South Korea's citizens flocked to the growing number of factory jobs in Seoul and other newly

"THE SCARIEST PLACE IN THE WORLD"?

When Bill Clinton visited the Korean Demilitarized Zone the U.S. president called it "one of the scariest places in the world." More than a million and a half armed soldiers guard it on both sides, all "ready to fight at a moment's notice," according to Don Oberdorfer, in his book *The Two Koreas*. Scattered throughout it is a "densely planted underground garden of deadly land mines," and therefore patrolling soldiers take care to stay on the "well-worn paths." One result of the DMZ's inhospitality is that it has become a sanctuary for wildlife. In between the razored and barbed wire that surround it is a "richly forested, unspoiled two-and-a-half-mile strip of land that stretches like a ribbon for 150 miles across the waist of the Korean peninsula. Here several hundred rare white-naped cranes stop over each spring and autumn in migration. . . . Amid a profusion of wildflowers, the birds join even rarer endangered red-crowned Manchurian cranes," which join "other year-round residents such as pheasant, wild pigs, black bears, and small Korean deer."

Seoul, the capital of South Korea, is a major exporter of manufactured goods. The city also boasts one of the highest standards of living in Asia.

industrial cities like Taegu and Kwangju. Seoul became a serious rival to the industrial and commercial centers of Japan, and its hardworking people enjoyed a steadily increasing standard of living. Just thirty-five years after the destruction of the Korean War, Seoul was awarded the honor of hosting the international Summer Olympic Games in 1988.

Air pollution from cars and factories as well as emissions from coal fires used to heat homes has been one downside of progress in Seoul. A vastly improved public transportation system has improved that situation, although some pollution problems remain.

Residents of Seoul and other South Korean cities enjoy one of the highest living standards in Asia. The country serves as a model for other countries trying to engineer the same sort of success. While South Korea has spent the last few decades working on a better future for itself, the past still holds great importance. For Koreans, that past began in 2333 B.C.

THE EARLIEST
KOREANS

Today's Koreans are part of two thousand years of recorded history. But archaeological finds go back much further, beginning in Siberia and Manchuria on the northern Asian continent. That is where the ancestors of modern-day Koreans are thought to have originated, most likely in Siberia, migrating into Manchuria, and then, in an effort to avoid more hostile tribes, down into the Korean peninsula that dangles between China and Japan in northeast Asia.

Evidence shows that the peninsula was occupied from about 3000 B.C. Koreans, though, give a more precise point in time as the beginning of their culture and heritage: 2333 B.C. It was then, according to ancient belief, that the half-human, half-divine Tan-gun founded the kingdom called Choson and began his reign over the Korean people. The mythical Tan-gun, whose ruling title was "Son of Heaven," is looked upon as the father of the Korean ethnic group, setting them apart from other Asian people, and his story still is celebrated today.

"Geography dealt Korea a particularly difficult role,"[1] Don Oberdorfer observes in his book *The Two Koreas: A Contemporary History*. Korea's two thousand-year recorded history tells of hundreds of invasions from its ambitious neighbors, as well as several periods of foreign occupation, with the three most recent being in the twentieth century. In particular, the split into two separate Koreas, an event recalled by many people living today, deeply wounded the spirit of the Korean people.

A COLLECTION OF CITY-STATES: CHINA'S EARLY INFLUENCE

Agriculture on the peninsula was underway perhaps by 1800 B.C., and fishing also was important for the people of Choson. By the eighth century B.C. bronze was used for items such as daggers; in the fourth century B.C. iron became the metal of choice. Iron probably was introduced by the Chinese, who by this time had become influential in the area: The Chinese also most likely introduced to Korea the production of rice. Such developments would often then pass from the peninsula eastward to Japan.

China became the established ruler of the area in 108 B.C., when it conquered the ancient Choson dynasty, which had developed into a collection of city-states. The new overlords

KOREAN INFLUENCE ON JAPAN

For fifty years, beginning at the end of the nineteenth century and lasting until the end of World War II, Japan was the master of Korea, and officially annexed it to its empire in 1910. It had been a menacing presence for three centuries before that. But one thousand years earlier, Japan had looked to the Korean city of Puyo, near the Yellow Sea, as the source of much of its own culture. Puyo was once part of the kingdom of Paekche, and it was from there that Buddhist monks set out to build the first monasteries in Japan. The first books seen in Japan were brought over by scribes from Korea, who then served as court historians to the Japanese monarchs. Korean scholars crossed the Sea of Japan to become teachers to its sons of royalty. Korean women were popular at the Japanese court for their skills such as embroidery. By the early ninth century, one-third of Japan's noble families were of Korean descent.

A Korean envoy presents an image of the Buddha to a Japanese ruler. During the fourth century, Japan adopted many aspects of Korean culture, including Buddhism.

set up a series of commanderies, or ruling districts, in the north part of the peninsula and stayed for several hundred years, using their more advanced technology and well-organized military and government to maintain control.

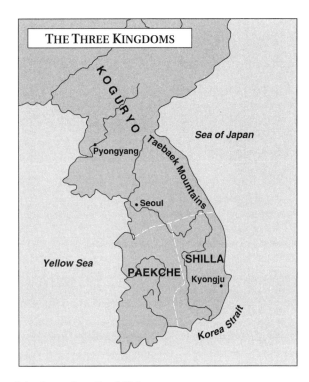

In the meantime, three kingdoms were forming in the modern-day Koreas. To the north, in A.D. 313, the kingdom known as Koguryo at last inflicted crippling defeats on the ruling Lolang dynasty, which had held power in the area for more than two hundred years. While Koguryo kept busy warring with China, another kingdom, Paekche, was building a power base of its own in the southwest corner of the peninsula, just as the kingdom of Shilla was along the eastern coast. It was also during this time that Buddhism made its way to the northern kingdom of Paekche near the end of the fourth century, and made an impact on Shilla by early in the sixth century.

During the fourth-century Three Kingdoms era, Korea served as a conduit in that part of the world for new ideas, such as Buddhism, and new technology. Another philosophy/religion that came from China was based on the teachings of a Chinese sage known to Westerners as Confucius. Confucianism would have much influence on Korean life up to the present day. The modern nations in that part of the world were not formed yet: for example, the people of Korea's southern coast and on what is today the Japanese island of Kyushu most likely shared a similar culture.

Each of the three kingdoms on the Korean peninsula strove to build and consolidate power, competing for territory in hopes of reigning over the entire peninsula. Many of the rulers practiced Buddhism, but ran their governments and their armies according to the principles of Confucius. Shilla put extra effort into training its young men for war, as well as in art and the Confucian virtue of obedience, which gave it a

ANCIENT CAPITALS

Today, Seoul is the capital of South Korea, and
has been a capital city for centuries. But there are other "capitals" in South Korea, too. Puyo, in central South Korea near the
Yellow Sea, was the capital of the kingdom of Paekche, and
relics of that era can be seen at the Puyo National Museum.
Kyongju, in southeast Korea, was quite important in its day
as the capital of the kingdom of Shilla. The Shilla devotion to
Buddhism is still preserved there in the form of artwork and
relics on display at the Kyongju National Museum. Pyongyang
was put back into service as a capital for North Korea, having
once been capital first of the old kingdom of Koguryo and
then of the Koryo dynasty.

military edge over the other two kingdoms. Shilla also developed a partnership with China's T'ang dynasty, against which
Koguryo was still battling. Koguryo, in fact, inflicted a crush-
ing defeat on the T'ang army in 612 and kept the enemy from
the north part of the peninsula for several decades. But Shilla
then teamed up with the T'ang to defeat Koguryo and Paekche
in 668, and it was from this point that Korea began its history
as a united country.

ONE COUNTRY, UNDER SHILLA

Though the Chinese had helped Shilla conquer Paekche and
Koguryo, Shilla soon turned its attention toward lone rule over
the peninsula, and completely expelled the Chinese from the
entire territory. Wars against invading Chinese armies lasted
another sixty years, until finally China gave up its claim on
the area. Ruling over the kingdom of Shilla was a small group
of aristocrats who could claim relations to the king. The capital of Shilla was in Kyongju, near the southeast coast and
across from present-day Japan.

With peace at hand, Shilla rulers were able to focus on the
advancement of agriculture. For example, reservoirs were
built to irrigate rice fields. Peasants received land allot-
ments, paying taxes to the government and local noble families in the form of crops or other products like walnuts, and
they planted mulberry trees for silkworms. A census from
Kyongju taken in the ninth century shows 178,936 households there, representing probably more than a half-million

people. The census also lists citizens' ages, gender, and material possessions. With this information the kings of Shilla could identify taxable property and estimate how much labor was available for construction projects such as Buddhist monuments.

THE IMPACT OF BUDDHISM

The kingdom of Shilla would rule the peninsula for more than two hundred sixty years, between the years 668 to 935; it reached its height of power and culture in the middle of the peaceful eighth century. Buddhism, installed as the official religion in about the year 700, was a main source of inspiration for artistic and cultural achievement, and its adherents wielded considerable political power as well.

The religion and philosophy known as Buddhism originated in India in the fifth and sixth centuries B.C. It is based on the teachings of Siddartha Gautama, an Indian prince who became known as the Buddha, or enlightened one. A follower of Buddha seeks nirvana, a state in which one has finally replaced one's worldly self with a completely spiritual self, and joins a supreme spirit.

Gautama himself did not worship a specific deity, or god; rather, he developed a set of spiritual goals that would help decrease human suffering. As Buddhism spread throughout Asia, however, it picked up "regional peculiarities," according to *A Handbook of Korea*. In Korea, the *Handbook* continues,

A modern Buddhist shrine testifies to the enduring legacy of this belief in Korea. Buddhism became the official faith of Shilla in about 700 and is still one of the main religions practiced in South Korea today.

"almost every Buddhist temple complex has a side chapel near the main worship hall containing a shrine to the mountain spirit [of that area, which is usually shown as] an old man with a pet tiger."[2]

THE INCREASING INFLUENCE OF CONFUCIANISM

Shilla was a prosperous kingdom, and with no wars to fight during the eighth century, education became a priority. Emphasis on scholarship was in line with Confucian teachings, and the National Confucian College opened its doors in 682. The establishment of this institution paved the way for centuries of peaceful coexistence between Confucianism and Buddhism. Confucianism laid the foundation for social behavior and governmental organization, while Buddhism served primarily spiritual needs and offered an approach to dealing with the supernatural considerably different from the shamanistic worship of earlier days.

Chinese philosopher Confucius (551–479 B.C.) developed a system of behavioral codes that shaped ancient and modern Korean society.

Shamanism revolves around the idea of powerful spirits guiding the activities of nature and people. A shaman is a person considered especially gifted in communicating with the spirits. So it was the shamans who conducted the ceremonies designed to convey to the spirits the needs of the people, such as rain for crops or animals to be hunted.

By the eighth century, the practice of shamanism was less widespread among educated Koreans, who hoped to receive, through scholarship, important positions within the government. Korea had borrowed from China the idea of using civil service examinations to choose the scholars who would contribute most to the country's cultural and political development. But in Korea, the all-important exam was open only to the highest classes of noble families, whereas in China, the exam was open to all. This strict policy in Korea, which blocked the lower aristocracy's chances for advancement, was to have far-reaching effects.

Conflicts between royalty and the different levels of aristocracy began to erode the power of the ruling class. Peasants felt increasing strain as they had to work harder to support the ever more luxurious lifestyle of the nobility, and rebellions against the king became more common. Finally, in 935, the Shilla kingdom came to an end at the hands of the victorious Koryo dynasty from the former region of Koguryo, and from which the name Korea eventually came.

A New Dynasty, Koryo, and its Cultural Achievements

Like Shilla, the Koryo dynasty based its government on Confucian ideals, using a civil service exam to choose influential scholars. At the core of the government was a council to the king; from that grew the aristocracy, or *yangban*, which included important families from a variety of regions for better representation. Other classes in Koryo society were free peasants, skilled workers, and slaves.

Enjoying a two hundred-year period of relative peace, the culture of Koryo flourished, spurred on by devotion to Buddha. As in the Shilla dynasty, both Confucianism and Buddhism remained influential in Koryo's culture. Many Buddhist temples were built, adorned with sculptures and paintings. Buddhist monasteries paid no taxes on their generous grants of land, and some became so wealthy that they formed their own armies to protect not only their temples but their land and their priceless works of art. Prominent Buddhist priests became tutors and advisers to royalty, and had much influence on government affairs.

In 1126, a huge fire caused the destruction of not only all the royal palace buildings but tens of thousands of books. To replace the books with more woodblock-printed volumes would have been expensive and very time-consuming. So, Korean administrators wondered, why not make books by means of movable type, just as coins were printed? This revolutionary idea was tested successfully, and by the middle of

CONFUCIAN ATTITUDES

It was during the Shilla era that Confucianism took root as the ethical basis of Korean national life, influencing government's relations to citizens and the behavior of individual citizens alike. The goal of Confucianism was to ensure an orderly society by defining each person's place in the system and making clear who was in charge in any situation. As in many other cultures, women were thought to require much protection, and in return the Confucian code of behavior imposed strict rules of obedience and loyalty on females.

Most of the restrictions fell on upper-class women who seldom showed themselves in public in daylight. The so-called protection of more privileged girls and young women included keeping them home, where they were taught to read, and away from schools. As recently as the nineteenth century, in Korea's first Christian churches, men and women sat on opposite sides of the church. The "female side" was concealed from the "male side" by a curtain of blankets, hung from lines, and the clergyman preached from the male side. Later, when young women were allowed to attend schools, largely because of the influence of foreign Christian missionaries, they at first could not face a male teacher; he would teach from behind a screen, or keep his back toward the class and face the blackboard.

Men could divorce their wives for nagging, for not being respectful enough to the husband's parents, or for exhibiting jealousy. Widows were discouraged from remarrying, because their children would acquire a new set of ancestors, resulting in the neglect of their biological father's ancestors. A rural widow who remained single was honored by a *yol*, or memorial tablet, in her village, but not until after she died.

the twelfth century, well before Johannes Gutenberg made
the same discovery in Europe, Koryo was using movable type
to print books. The new printing system produced books
about philosophy, history, government regulations, etiquette,
music theory, and even an encyclopedia.

In the meantime, the *yangban* had grown both larger and
argumentative, weakening the power of the king. In 1170
military officers, who were excluded from the aristocracy,
staged a coup. This sudden overthrow of the government resulted in a sixty-year period of military rule.

There were attacks from Japan all over the peninsula, and
in 1231 the Mongols, who had conquered China, invaded
Koryo on their way to Japan. Many lives were lost and much
property was destroyed; the royal court and its officials fled
the capital city, which was just north of today's Demilitarized
Zone. After several years, during which the Mongols were
weakened by internal strife, the people of Koryo were able to
drive out the invaders.

But that did not bring peace. The visible wealth and power
of many Buddhist monasteries came under increasing criticism as contradictory to the Buddha's teachings of humility,
simplicity, and sharing with others. There was also a practical objection: When Mongol forces entered the peninsula in
1231, prayers to Buddha had been ineffective in repelling
the invasion.

Combined with rumblings of disapproval of a religious elite
was popular dissatisfaction with high taxes. Peasant rebellions
became more common, as did attacks by Japanese pirates.

A NEW LEADER TAKES CONTROL

From the military came General Yi Song-gye, who not only
took care of the pirate problem but went on to seize control of
the entire peninsula. The dynasty he founded in 1392 would
last until the twentieth century and would see Korea through
a variety of social changes. It would also witness the country's very unwilling entry, in the nineteenth century, into the
international political arena.

3

CHOSON:
A FIVE-HUNDRED-
YEAR DYNASTY

The new political era begun in Korea by General Yi looked both backward and forward. Yi at first put a king of his own choice on the Korean throne, but then decided to do the job himself. He brought back the ancient name Choson for the kingdom as he also looked to China for a model of government. Seoul was established as the capital city.

In Choson, Confucianism remained the ruling philosophy, while Buddhism slowly fell out of favor. *A Handbook of Korea* relates that in the Confucian idea of good government, "the bureaucracy was to act as the agent of the monarch's will,"[3] since, theoretically, the monarch, or king/queen, would strive to be fair to all subjects and follow the advice of the court's Confucian scholars. New Confucian schools were established, such as the National Confucian Academy in Seoul. Its Korean name is Songgyungwan (*song* meaning maturity, *gyun* meaning harmony, and *gwan* meaning institution), and it still exists today. Movable type, used for printing Buddhist texts in the 1300s, was put to use in printing Confucian literature by the early fifteenth century.

THE *YANGBAN* AND OTHER SOCIAL CLASSES

General Yi redistributed land among the nobility, who in turn collected rent from the peasant farmers in the form of half of their crops. The *yangban*, made up now of civilian and military elites, had enough power to check the monarch's absolute control over the country. The *yangban* were very protective of Confucian tradition and ideals, and strove to counter any leanings toward Buddhism on the part of the monarch. Participation in Choson government was limited to those who had passed the examinations that only the *yangban* were eligible to take, and that group continued to control the social hierarchy, allowing little or no upward

ROBIN HOOD, KOREAN STYLE

By the 1500s, the *yangban* class had expanded, and the private schools they founded had increased the number of young men qualified to take part in the country's ruling bureacracy. To support the ever-growing nobility, peasant farmers and laborers paid ever-growing taxes. To help alleviate their suffering, a Robin Hood–type character named Im Kkok-chong would steal food the government was storing in granaries and gave it back to the peasants who had grown it; he robbed members of the *yangban* and distributed their money to the poor.

Im Kkok was captured and beheaded in 1562. But his life story was cherished among Koreans and eventually inspired a popular novel, *The Tale of Hong Kil-tong*, as well as a television series in the 1980s.

mobility of lower classes, or the illegitimate children of *yangban*. Various noble families, intent on maintaining the influence of their clans at court, established private schools to prepare their sons for the government exams.

Below royalty and the *yangban* on the social ladder were the *chung'in*, or skilled workers such as clerks, scribes, doctors, or artisans. Then came the *ajon*, or petty clerks, whose jobs were hereditary and who served the government bureaucracy. Most Korean people were *sangmin*, or commoners who farmed or provided a variety of low-skilled labor for the upper classes. Slavery was practiced in Korea, mostly by the government, but in some private families as well. Slavery lasted in Korea until into the nineteenth century, and was more widespread than in China or Japan.

THE REMARKABLE KING SEJONG

It was under the king Sejong in the first half of the fifteenth century that the Yi dynasty made its most lasting contributions to Korean history. Sejong reigned from 1418 to 1450; he oversaw the development in the 1440s of a Korean alphabet called *han-gul*. Much less complicated than the Chinese system of writing, *han-gul* made reading possible for a variety of people, not just the upper classes. When works written with the new alphabet were printed by means of movable type, Korean literature became much more prominent, though Chinese characters continued to be used in government documents.

Sejong's interest in science led to other inventions, including the pluviometer, which measures rainfall and which made its debut in Europe almost two hundred years later. Under his sponsorship astronomical maps and clocks were developed, and information was published about the seven known planets (Korea already had one of the world's oldest observatories).

In the early part of his reign, Sejong suppressed the practice of Buddhism. No more temples were built, and lands owned by many wealthy Buddhist monasteries were confiscated, returning the property to the king's tax base and lessening the power of the monks. However, later in the Choson dynasty, Buddhism would again enjoy a prominent place in Korean culture.

Sejong's long, stable, and prosperous reign was followed by the brief reigns of his successors, under whom the *yangban* expanded its influence through its system of private schools. To balance that power, one of Sejong's successors put forth the theory that royalty ruled by divine mandate, since Korean kings were descended from Tan-gun, the Son-of-Heaven ruler. To compensate for the new royal mandate, members of the military elite were given generous land grants, but nonmilitary *yangban* received land grants only for the time they held government offices, rather than for life. Buddhism inched its way back into favor again; the Office for Publication of Buddhist Scriptures was opened, and works by Chinese and Japanese Buddhists were translated into the Korean language.

JAPAN TRIES TO CONQUER WESTERN NEIGHBORS

As the numbers, status, and power of the *yangban* waxed and waned, and as technological and cultural advances changed everyday life for many Koreans, other changes were afoot that would make an impact on the peninsula: Choson's neighbors were looking for ways to increase their power, too, and Korea was one step along the way. Though the kings of the Yi dynasty tried to isolate their country and remain self-sufficient (hence the nickname "the Hermit Kingdom," which stuck for centuries), wars often were necessary to maintain independence. At the end of the sixteenth century, the Japanese military leader Toyotomi Hideyoshi began eyeing China as a land to be conquered.

Hideyoshi approached the Koreans for help with his plan. When they refused, Hideyoshi made Korea his first point of attack in 1592. The Japanese soldiers had something the defending Koreans did not—matchlock guns—and Hideyoshi was in Seoul within two weeks. The invasion was devastating to Choson; landmark buildings and artworks were destroyed, and agriculture was disrupted. Korea was fortunate in having a military leader of its own, Admiral Yi Sun-shin, who routed the Japanese from Korea in a series of naval battles that ended with the sinking of 250 Japanese ships along the southern coast of Korea.

Yi helped develop the world's first ironclad warships, which the Koreans called *kobukson*, or "turtle ships": The ships were plated with iron and shaped somewhat like a turtle shell. When China's Ming dynasty came to Korea's aid, the Japanese retreated, but returned five years later. That invasion ended with the sudden death of Hideyoshi, but Korea never fully recovered from the Japanese attacks of the late sixteenth century.

A Japanese artist's illustration of Japan's 1592 invasion of Korea. Led by Toyotomi Hideyoshi, Japanese soldiers dealt a severe blow to Choson.

"TURTLE SHIPS"

"Necessity is the mother of invention," goes an old saying, and one good example of that is the ironclad ships designed by Korea's hero admiral, Yi Sun-shin.

Korea's coast was under heavy attack by the Japanese navy in 1592. The idea for an iron-covered ship had been suggested almost two hundred years earlier, but the idea did not become a reality until it was urgently needed. The "turtle boat" that Yi invented to repel the attacks was unlike any other ship. About one hundred feet long and twenty-five feet wide, the slave-propelled ships were sided with iron which repelled cannonballs and fire-tipped arrows; spikes jutting out from the ship made it difficult for other vessels to get close enough to board. Twenty-six portholes allowed for cannon fire from the ship's side, and a wood fire was kept burning to cloud the turtle ship in smoke during battle. Admiral Yi's ships were a key element in sending the Japanese army home in defeat in 1592, and he is considered to be one of world history's great admirals. Today, there is an enormous shrine dedicated to him at Asan, as well as a statue of him on Seoul's main thoroughfare.

Much farmable land had been destroyed, and thus much of the tax base. To raise money, the government began selling noble titles conferring *yangban* status, which, as a result, became less and less valuable with each generation. Choson's economic struggles were made worse by invasions from the powerful Manchus, who conquered China in 1644 and were the founders of the Ch'ing dynasty, which lasted until 1911. Yet despite Manchurian domination, the Korean government continued its efforts to keep the country isolated, for its own protection and in an attempt to rebuild itself. But both internal and external forces ensured that the once tightly bound social structure would continue to unravel.

THE CHALLENGE OF CHRISTIANITY

Early in the Yi dynasty the *yangban* had been able to maintain its status, but upward mobility became commonplace in the seventeenth century. Rich merchants and even ambitious peasants could now buy that once-exclusive status, and intermarriage between social classes took place regularly. Writers and scholars spoke of doing away with class status, and ridiculed the *yangban*. Other social changes came from outside the Korean borders in the seventeenth century: Christian missionaries from Europe had arrived in China, and their ideas were eventually introduced into Korea.

The first known Westerners in Korea were Dutch, seventeenth-century survivors of a shipwreck off Chejudo. They were held captive for years but escaped at last to return to Europe. One survivor produced what historian David Steinberg calls "the first western account of Korea."[4] The seventeenth century also saw the arrival of Roman Catholic Jesuit missionaries, who not only won some converts, but touched off fears that ideas introduced by Christianity might lead to unwanted changes in the Confucian way of life.

Perhaps as a reaction to the new influx of Western ideas, interest in Korean culture grew among a group of Confucian scholars known as the Sirhak. While the movement inspired new works of art and literature based on Korean subjects or history, its authors' sometimes critical analysis of Korean history was not well received by the country's leaders. The rulers of Korea continued their stance of isolation and ignored the Sirhak's suggestions for Korean self-improvement in the areas of commerce or industry.

But in spite of self-imposed isolation and wars with Manchuria and Japan, Korea made advances in the seventeenth century. Farmers learned how to transplant rice and use fertilizer, which meant more food for a growing population. Coins became widely used, enabling commerce to expand. Artisans began to form guilds, and the merchant class grew while the power and prestige of the *yangban* continued its decline.

By the nineteenth century, the *yangban* class made up more than 70 percent of the population in some areas, since almost anyone could buy or forge a genealogy, or claim to a family line, which was needed to be considered *yangban*. Slaves, on the other hand, went from being almost one-third of the population at the end of the seventeenth century to a minute percentage by the mid-1800s.

During the latter part of the Choson kingdom, the peasant classes still were exploited by those whom they served as farmers or laborers, and peasant wars erupted in the first half of the 1800s. Moreover, Roman Catholic missionaries were helping to establish schools for young women, further weakening popular adherence to Confucian principles of submission to one's superiors in a rigid social order. There was some

PROTECTOR CHINA

Early in its history, Korea was under the rule of the Chinese, who were eventually expelled by the Shilla dynasty. But in the next millennium, during the Yi dynasty, China again took on the role of protector. Korea's kings called their own shots, and Korean politics operated independently, but awareness that China's military might would be used against them inhibited Korea's other neighbors from swallowing Korea up. Japan tried to conquer Korea late in the sixteenth century, but only because it was on its way to invade China. By the nineteenth century, China's military power in Asia was weakened sufficiently to permit Western nations to force treaties on Korea. In addition, Japan's gradual takeover of the peninsula became complete, and lasted until the end of the Second World War.

early persecution of Catholics in Korea, but heavy-handed attempts to suppress the religion came later. In 1866, for example, several French priests and thousands of Korean Catholics were executed. Christianity continued to grow in Korea, though secretly.

"HERMIT" ERA COMES TO AN END

By that time, Korea was being dragged into international relationships, as were other Asian countries: America's Admiral Perry arrived in Japan in the 1850s. England, Russia, and the United States made their intentions to trade with Korea quite clear. Twice, American naval ships tried sailing up rivers to reach Korean cities, in 1866 and 1871. Both attempts were repelled by the Koreans, but at the cost of hundreds of lives.

Japan showed increasing interest in Korea, rich in natural resources and plentiful rice harvests. Russia also came calling, in need of a warm-water port. England gave Korea attention because it wanted to inhibit Russian influence there. China, supposedly Korea's ruling parent since the 1600s, was no longer strong enough to prevent outside interest in Korea. In the 1860s the ruling Korean prince tried to shield the Hermit Kingdom from outside interest, but isolation was no longer possible. Under the direction of this ruler, Korea signed a treaty of commerce with the United States, which seemed the nation least likely to turn Korea into a colony.

But that treaty did nothing to prevent Japanese designs on Korea. Japan positioned troops and warships in the Sea of Japan near Pusan. Under this threat, a treaty was signed between the two countries and a Japanese bank was opened in Pusan, giving Japan access to Korean "rice, soy beans, cattle hides and alluvial gold at incredibly low prices."[5] The Japanese suspected the Korean queen Min of seeking help from China and arranged for her assassination. The Chinese, whose assistance Min had indeed been trying to obtain, did not come to her defense.

ASIAN WARS FOLLOWED BY JAPANESE DOMINATION

The Korean government still wrangled with rebellious peasants whose lives were made very difficult by crop failures. Peaceful demonstrations against an oppressive government and foreign influence proved futile, and so peasants formed their own armies. The peasants had not foreseen, however, that Japan would use their puny threat as an excuse to enter Korea militarily, claiming the necessity to stabilize the peninsula. It was the presence of the Japanese troops in Korea that set off war between China and Japan in 1894. The Chinese suffered a harsh defeat in what became known as the Sino-Japanese War, and Korea was released from domination by its mainland neighbor. But Japan was closing in aggressively, strengthening its economic control of Korea.

The Korean people tried to hold their own against the Japanese, who slowly attempted to overpower the Korean culture as well as the economy. For example, it became illegal for Korean men to wear their hair in the traditional Korean topknot, which had been the custom for centuries. The Koreans did not accept Japanese dominion passively, and formed resistance groups. Amid the turmoil, Russia saw a chance to move into Korea as a helper: After Queen Min's assassination, the Korean king took refuge aboard a Russian warship anchored at Inch'on. He eventually returned to the palace at Seoul and proclaimed Korea to be an independent empire in 1897. Japan agreed to allow the Russians to remain at port as long as they did not interfere with Japan's activities in Korea. Those two countries held discussions about dividing Korea to share its resources and ports, but did not act on the idea since both Japan and Russia were aiming for control of Korea, not cooperation with a rival.

Japanese forces enter China during the Sino-Japanese War. China was defeated in 1895 and Korea fell under Japanese domination.

Russia moved into Manchuria early in the twentieth century, still looking for a warm-water port, but too close for comfort. The Russo-Japanese War broke out in 1904. Literally in the middle of the conflict was Korea; at that point Japan took complete control of the country. U.S. president Theodore Roosevelt intervened in the Russo-Japanese War, helping to end it in 1905; for those efforts Roosevelt won the Nobel Peace Prize. But as part of the treaty agreement, Japan was left in charge of Korea. The United States had economic interests in the Philippine Islands, and Japan agreed to ignore the American presence in the Pacific if America would not move to oust Japan from Korea.

The Japanese officially took control of Korea on Feb. 1, 1906, and annexed it to their empire in 1910, thus beginning a painful era for the Korean people. In the forty years Japan spent in charge of Korea, it enforced many measures aimed at wiping out Korean culture, language, and history and remaking it into a part of the Japanese empire. Japanese citizens immigrated to Korea and were given much of the best land. By the 1940s, more than 700,000 Japanese civilians lived in Korea. Japanese military police kept control over the Korean populace, who had no intention of giving up their heritage.

In 1919 there was a nationwide demonstration in Korea against the Japanese, and a Declaration of Korean Independence, dated March 1, was read aloud in Seoul:

> We do hereby declare and proclaim that Korea is an independent country and that the Koreans are a free people. . . . We declare this with an authority supported by a five-thousand-year-old history. . . . Let us press forward courageously toward the light ahead."[6]

The Japanese reminded the Koreans of their authority less than a month later: In a small village, about thirty Koreans were ordered to gather in a church. Doors and windows were locked, and the building was set afire. The world learned of this atrocity through Christian missionaries who visited the village shortly afterward.

As the Korean independence movement became better organized, a Manchuria-based provisional Korean government (which claimed to be the real govenment of Korea) appealed to other world powers for help. But many of those countries, such as Great Britain, had colonies of their own, and were reluctant to interfere with Japan's control of Korea. By the 1930s, about half of Korea's rice production was being shipped to Japan, while many Koreans neared starvation.

Crowds mourn at the funeral of the last Yi dynasty ruler, who reigned over Korea until its annexation by Japan. Though officially subjects of the Japanese empire, Koreans resisted Japanese attempts to stifle their culture.

In the late 1930s Japan used Korea as a base for an invasion into Manchurian China. As one consequence of this operation, Korea was outfitted with modern factories for heavy and light machinery, and its ports as well as roads and railways were improved. After the end of the World War II, when the Japanese were expelled in defeat, this new infrastructure would prove very advantageous for Koreans. But in the meantime, Korean citizens were drafted first to work in Japanese industry, and then to serve in its army as Japan fought against the United States and other Allies between 1941 and 1945.

Midway through the war, in 1943, Korea received the backing it had sought decades earlier, when the United States and Great Britain publicly stated their support for an independent Korea. Japan surrendered to the United States in August 1945, and Korea was officially liberated. But peace, and independence, remained a long way off.

An Independent South Korea, a Divided Peninsula

At the end of World War II, Korea traded domination by Japan for occupation by the major players in the upcoming cold war: the United States and the Soviet Union. The two powerful nations had been uneasy allies during the war, but their experiences of the conflict were very different.

The Soviets, who had taken a tremendous battering from the Germans and suffered over 20 million casualties, did not enter the war against Japan until after the bombing of Hiroshima in August 1945. But by declaring itself an enemy of Japan in the closing weeks of the war, the USSR was able to present itself to Korea as a "liberator."

The Soviets and the Americans had agreed to split the country at about the 38th parallel, with each occupier playing a role in helping Korea get back on its feet. The division, which was performed without consulting any Korean officials, was considered temporary. But it was soon apparent that, whereas the United States meant to stay only long enough to help get a new Korean government up and running, the Soviet Union had no intention of leaving the north. Two governments were formed: the Republic of Korea in the south in 1948, and, soon after, the Democratic People's Republic of Korea in the north.

Division Leads to Civil War

U.S. officials involved in engineering the split were successful in keeping the capital city of Seoul south of the 38th parallel. Pyongyang, once the capital of Koryo, became the capital of the new North Korea, which also had most of the peninsula's natural resources, as well as most of the aging industrial centers that had been built by the Japanese.

The United Nations recommended that free elections for a new Korean government be held throughout the country,

*Syngman Rhee,
president of South
Korea from 1948 to
1960, was the first
elected head of state
in Korean history.*

but voting took place only in the southern half. A Soviet-organized government led by a young Kim Il Sung ran North Korea. In the south, the much older Syngman Rhee became president of the Republic of Korea, the first elected head of state in the history of the peninsula. The UN recognized the Republic of Korea—that is, South Korea—as the legitimate government of Korea, since it had complied with the recommendation to hold free elections. Much later, in 1991, the world body recognized both the Republic of Korea and its northern counterpart, as legitimate governments.

Rhee was known for his appeals to world powers for help during the Japanese occupation; like other Koreans, he was unhappy with a divided country, and sought help for an invasion into North Korea, intending to someday lead a reunited nation.

The Communist government of the north had the same idea but made the first move: On June 25, 1950, its army crossed the 38th parallel and invaded South Korea, and within three days Seoul was in North Korean hands. The South Korean government already had moved south and set up temporary headquarters in Pusan. North Korea's invasion drew international attention; the U.S. military returned to the peninsula, leading a UN force of troops from sixteen nations as well as South Korea. North Korea was aided by neighboring Communist countries China and the Soviet Union. By early autumn of 1950, Seoul was recaptured from the North Koreans, and during most of the war the battle lines remained near the 38th parallel.

After three years of intense fighting, the United States began negotiating for a truce with North Korea. The United States, North Korea, and China signed an armistice, or ceasefire agreement, on July 27, 1953. Syngman Rhee refused to sign any agreement in which Korea remained divided. But he did finally consent to the truce as long as the United States agreed to continue defending South Korea with troops and arms. Honoring this agreement, American soldiers have been stationed in South Korea, alongside the Demilitarized Zone, for more than forty years.

THE KOREAN WAR: MACARTHUR'S CRUCIAL MOVE AT INCH'ON

When tanks and troops came spilling south over the 38th parallel from North Korea before dawn on June 25, 1950, it was a complete surprise to the south. By the end of the summer of 1950, North Korea occupied most of the peninsula except for the southeast corner surrounding Pusan. South Korea was outarmed and outnumbered; General Douglas MacArthur, who had commanded the U.S. efforts against Japan in World War II, was put in charge of the UN force, which at this point consisted of South Korean and inexperienced American soldiers.

The war looked bleak for the south in September 1950. The UN troops were cornered inside the "Pusan Perimeter" and, with the Sea of Japan behind them, there was no more room for retreat. MacArthur had a daring proposal: He suggested a major naval attack at Inch'on, a port city just southwest of Seoul. It was the only way, MacArthur argued, to recapture Seoul, and it would force the North Koreans to fight in two places at the same time. MacArthur's plan was not popular with his superiors in Washington, however. Inch'on, they argued, had no beaches, only piers and seawalls. But most of all, the tides at Inch'on were the second strongest and highest in the world, making any kind of naval landing risky. One general called the strategy's success a "5,000-to-one-shot." But they finally agreed to it, and plans were set for September 15.

MacArthur's plan was, indeed, a success; this time the surprise element worked in South Korea's favor. The UN troops quickly advanced on land, and in less than ten days, Seoul was retaken. North Korea's army to the south panicked, trying to get back north before being trapped between UN troops, who managed to push their way into North Korea almost as far as China. Though Chinese troops would come to North Korea's aid later in the fall and push back the UN army, the front lines of the war remained near the 38th parallel, and Seoul was kept in South Korean hands. And though there was no victor when the fighting ended in July 1953, the outcome of the Korean War, and the modern history of the peninsula, might have been very different if not for MacArthur's landing at Inch'on, considered one of the most effective military moves in history.

The 38th parallel marked the border between U.S.-occupied South Korea and Soviet-occupied North Korea after World War II. It was also the site of much of the fighting during the Korean War.

AN UPHILL CLIMB FROM WAR'S DEVASTATION

South Korea was practically in ruins from the Korean civil war. When the Republic of Korea was formed in 1948, it was among the poorest countries in the world, its people's standard of living long depressed by the Japanese. The Korean War made the already desperate situation worse.

Four hundred thousand soldiers fighting under the UN banner died, two-thirds of them South Korean. Fifty-four thousand American soldiers died, and 103,000 were wounded. North Korea lost more than a million soldiers, and more than a million Korean civilians died throughout the peninsula. The majority of buildings were destroyed, north and south. Tension between the two sides was such that another outbreak of war seemed possible at any time.

Having been ruled by the Japanese for more than forty years, and by Confucian-influenced monarchs before that, South Korea had no experience with any form of democracy. Syngman Rhee's government sought strict control of the South Korean population, and showed little respect for democratic principles or civil liberties. Rhee changed the constitution to allow himself to remain in office longer, and presidential elections, especially in 1960, were notoriously corrupt. University students led marches throughout the country to protest electoral abuses; the demonstrations spread to Seoul, and many students lost their lives at the hands of the police there. Rhee finally resigned his office and left Korea in 1960, dying in exile a few years later.

A MILITARY COMMANDER SEIZES CONTROL

The government structure was chaotic for the next year; Yun Po-son held the office of president until a military coup in 1961 led by Major General Park Chung Hee.

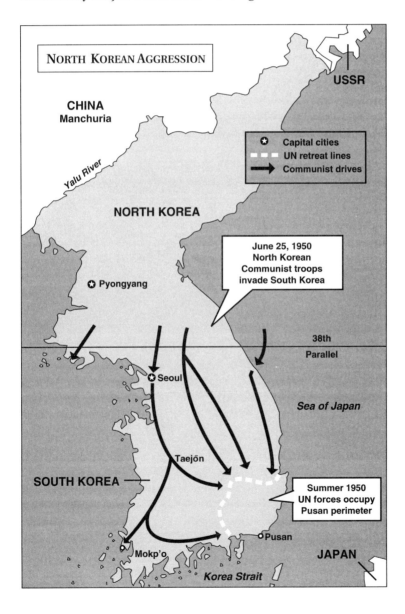

Park, who received his military training from the Japanese during their occupation, established the Korean Central Intelligence Agency. Like Rhee, he rewrote the constitution in his favor. Park was elected president of South Korea in 1971, the first time since 1960 that elections had been held. He centralized his own power by calling for martial law, saying a strong public military presence was necessary because South Korea might be under attack at any time from North Korea. Newspapers and other media were strictly controlled by the government. Thus Park created a dictatorship in South Korea, outlawing any form of protest. With his Japanese military training and his rigid interpretation of the Confucian respect for order, Park had little interest in democracy or Western-style civil liberties.

Yet, in recent years, a majority of South Koreans polled by a Seoul newspaper remembered Park as the best president in

More than a million Korean civilians were killed during the Korean War. The devastation of this war left South Korea severely impoverished.

the country's history. It was under his long and strict control of the country (1961 to 1979) that South Korea began its climb out of grinding poverty. As he once said, "All around me I could find little hope. . . . I had to destroy, once and for all, the vicious circle of poverty and economic stagnation" to secure for South Koreans "decent living standards."[7]

Park sought friendly relations with Japan, a very unpopular move with fellow South Koreans, but useful in winning much financial aid and investment from the Japanese. With economic progress as the main goal, the country built a steel mill and laid a cross-peninsula highway. South Korea received another important boost in the 1960s and '70s when contracts to manufacture military supplies came its way, as a reward for sending Korean troops to fight alongside U.S. forces in Vietnam.

Though a dictatorial and corrupt president, Park Chung Hee is credited with leading South Korea to economic recovery.

CORRUPTION CATCHES UP WITH THE PRESIDENT

Park's administration degenerated into lawlessness in later years. For example, he had one of his most outspoken critics kidnapped in 1972 and nearly murdered. U.S. intervention saved the life of the opposing politician, the popular Kim Dae Jung from Kwangju. Park also approved an attempt to bribe U.S. members of Congress a few years later in exchange for support for his presidency, touching off the American scandal known as Korea-gate.

But Park himself, unlike his counterpart Kim Il Sung in North Korea, never became wealthy as president. "He usually had a simple bowl of Korean noodles for lunch and ate rice mixed with barley, to save on rice,"[8] writes Don Oberdorfer. Coming from a rural background, Park was attentive to the needs of the peasant farmers. When he took over the government, nearly half of Korean families lived in abject poverty; less than 10 percent did at the end of Park's eighteen-year presidency.

Nevertheless, Park made many enemies with his dictatorial leadership, and public protests became more frequent. He was assassinated by a Korean CIA official and onetime close friend in October 1979.

ANOTHER MILITARY LEADER GRABS THE REINS

Within weeks of Park's assassination, another general stepped up to fill the vacuum: backed by the military, Chun Doo Hwan pushed aside the interim president, Choi Kyu Hah, and took over the government. Like Park, Chun had little taste for Western democracy and ran the country much as he might have commanded a branch of the military.

As a young Korean army officer, Chun had spent some time at American military bases; he spoke English well and felt comfortable around Americans. But the United States had little influence on Korean politics; the number of American soldiers guarding the DMZ had been decreased, replaced by a stronger Korean military presence there. And by 1980, South Korea was much more financially independent.

Its citizens wanted to become more politically independent, too, and student-organized protest rallies against martial law and in favor of presidential elections drew thousands of participants. In the meantime, Chun ordered the arrest of Kim Dae Jung, by now a national hero for opposing South Korea's totalitarian governments. When massive protests over Kim's arrest broke out in his home region of Kwangju in May 1980, Korean soldiers arrived on the scene to maintain order. Chun's troops used clubs to beat not only protesters, but bus riders, shopkeepers, even families in the area by chance.

REFORESTATION

Away from the large cities, South Korea's forests add their own beauty to the mountainous countryside. But much of today's scenic forests are the result of an intense reforestation (or tree-planting) effort during the 1960s, when it was realized that forested areas had become drastically scarce.

At first Koreans placed blame on Japanese lumbermen who, during the occupation years, might have helped themselves to too many trees. And the destruction of the Korean War did not help the situation. But it was actually Korea's wood-burning *ondol* heating system that was doing in the trees. As a remedy, oil became more widely used for the under-the-floor *ondol* heating, and trees were planted on millions of acres, bringing the density of forests back up to what they might have been under kings of Shilla or Choson.

Rather than be intimidated, the townspeople fought back against the soldiers, who withdrew and closed off the city.

Several days later, army forces moved into the city in the middle of the night. The army estimated the number of resulting deaths at 240, but Kwangju residents claimed that far more civilians had been killed by army troops. The Kwangju uprising was not soon forgotten by South Koreans, and further stained Chun's presidency.

Riot police in Kwangju form a human barrier to block the way of demonstrators protesting Kim Dae Jung's arrest. The 1980 Kwangju uprising resulted in the death of hundreds of civilians.

MARTIAL RULE BY A "CIVILIAN" CHUN

Chun attempted to smooth over the situation by retiring from the military and running for president as a civilian later in 1980. But the people of South Korea had little to cheer about: Chun also abolished the republic's National Assembly and instead set up the National Conference for Unification, a rubber-stamp body that approved all of his actions. In another change of the constitution, there was no direct election for president. Chun was made president by the government body he had formed, and promised to step down in seven years.

Meanwhile, Kim Dae Jung, whom Chun still feared as a rival for power, was accused and convicted of planning the Kwangju uprising. He was sentenced to death, but again American friends came to his rescue. In 1981 newly elected U.S. president Ronald Reagan invited Chun to Washington and held a reception for him at the White House. But the invitation came with a price tag: State Department officials requested Kim's life be spared. As added incentive to spare Kim, Chun was promised that the number of American troops stationed in South Korea would be increased.

Public dissatisfaction continued to increase. Periodically since the Korean War, incidents of aggression toward South Korea from the north had occurred at the DMZ. But by the 1980s the situation between the two Koreas appeared less threatening, and it seemed less necessary to keep South Korean citizens under military rule. The middle class was

TUNNELS TO SOUTH KOREA

In his book *The Two Koreas*, Don Oberdorfer tells of several remarkable feats of tunnel digging on the part of the North Koreans. This activity was first noticed in November 1974, when South Korean soldiers discovered a tunnel from North Korea burrowing through the Demilitarized Zone and exiting in South Korea, and through which hundreds of soldiers could be moved each hour. In fact, tunneling had been in high gear during unification and "peace" talks, in case the North Koreans wanted to initiate a "lightning attack" or sneak in spies.

A defector to the south from North Korea brought with him much information about several tunnels. One, simply called "tunnel number two," was "an extraordinary engineering feat, . . . constructed through solid granite more than fifty yards below ground," and could have channeled ten thousand men per hour, writes Oberdorfer. The tunnels were the subject of much publicity, as well as protests to the North Korean government from South Korea and the United States. Nevertheless, "the sounds of digging continued to be detected under the surface of the DMZ," and new tunnels were detected as recently as 1990, leaving no doubt about North Korea's aggressive intentions.

South Korean soldiers patrol a tunnel dug from North Korea to South Korea through the Demilitarized Zone.

growing and, better educated than ever, wanted a stronger voice in its own government. Never shy about protesting unfairness from government leaders, the South Korean people in the 1980s increased their demands for a modern, open government that operated under at least some democratic principles, such as free elections and a free press. No matter how hard Chun came down on protesters with martial law and soldiers patrolling the streets, demonstrations against his policies continued, and grew.

As he neared the end of his term, which he had promised would be 1987, Chun felt pressured to allow a peaceful transfer of power take place. Even his wife and children pleaded that cause with him. But Chun hesitated to hand over the reins of government in light of plans for the 1988 Summer Olympic Games, which were to be held in Seoul.

The games were much anticipated by South Koreans as a way of showcasing not only their unique Asian heritage and culture but the astounding economic and technological progress that had taken place on the southern half of the Korean peninsula in just thirty years. It was Park Chung Hee who had begun lobbying for the games shortly before his death in 1979. He hoped such an event would not only give South Korea a positive place in the public eye but help establish diplomatic and business relations with more countries around the world.

A TRUE ELECTION FOR PRESIDENT

As the time for the games neared, in 1987 Chun announced that he would step down and that his close friend and former general, Roh Tae Woo, would be a "candidate" for president. As the government was then structured, the declaration of Roh's candidacy ensured that he would be elected. Thus, Chun believed, there was little chance that a new, unpredictable president would assume office just when the world was watching Korea during the Olympics. But huge and sometimes violent protests broke out, with thousands of Korean citizens demanding a truly free election. In response, Roh agreed to run in a free election. The decision astonished Koreans because by now Roh's party was very unpopular. The two other prominent candidates, one of whom was Kim Dae Jung, split the opposition vote, however, and Roh was elected president in December 1987.

Once elected, Roh relaxed the laws restricting speech and the media. He also reached out to establish relations with Communist countries in Eastern Europe, a policy that heightened North Korea's sense of insecurity. For example, North Korea bitterly resented South Korea's decision to give Hungary a $625 million loan in exchange for full diplomatic relations. In 1990 South Korea entered into economic and diplomatic relations with the Soviet Union, which had once helped North Korea in its goal of conquering the south but was turning away from its twentieth-century experiment with communism. By 1992 China, too, established full diplomatic relations with South Korea, a goal Roh had worked toward since becoming president. China, in fact, encouraged more dialogue between North and South Korea, which had been sporadic for twenty years.

Two Nonmilitary Presidents

In 1993 Kim Young Sam became president of South Korea, the first nonmilitary president since Syngman Rhee. Kim, in fact, had been a vocal opponent of the military presidencies of Park and Chun, having served time in prison, though he was not as famous a dissident as his political opponent, Kim Dae Jung.

The presidency of Kim Young Sam coincided with a difficult time for South Korea, and as his term neared an end in 1997, the country's economic situation was revealed to be quite desperate. Several large companies were saved from failure only when they received a loan from an international fund, a bailout that the proud Koreans considered a national disgrace. Kim's popularity rating among South Koreans was below 10 percent.

As 1997 came to a close, a familiar figure became South Korea's leader: Kim Dae Jung, whose life former presidents Park and Chun had tried to end, was elected president at age seventy-two. A veteran of South Korea's political struggles, Kim still limps from one attempt on his life that occurred when he was a serious rival to Park Chung Hee in the early 1970s. Just a decade before his election, South Korea's newspapers were not allowed to mention Kim's name.

Citizens in Kim Dae Jung's home town of Kwangju rejoiced openly at Kim's election. It is thought that the new President Kim will relax more of the laws that still keep some political

*Kim Young Sam
served as president
of South Korea
from 1993 to 1997.*

prisoners behind bars, and continue to allow more open dissent, or criticism, from the public. The election of Kim Dae Jung, whose home district (the province of South Chŏlla) was once looked down upon as backward, appears to be another step toward democracy, and away from the rigid past, for South Korea.

5

THE ARTS IN KOREA

From court dances choreographed by long-ago dynasties to modern karaoke rooms in public shopping centers, the artistic culture of South Korea embraces tradition along with the newest fads, and without blinking blends East and West. For example, Korean folk dancing is as popular as European ballet, and a Beethoven symphony is as likely to be attended as a concert featuring traditional Korean instruments.

Although the arts of China and Japan have often overshadowed those of Korea, South Koreans are very proud of their artistic heritage. As in religion and technology, throughout history Korea often served as a cultural link between those two countries, as well. Centuries of wars and invasions resulted in the destruction of many of Korea's cultural relics, such as architecture or pieces of fine art. So today, the government protects what remains as cultural treasures, which can be an art object, a musical instrument, a building, or even a living person whose talent and achievement in a certain artistic field has won the title of National Living Treasure as well as a certain amount of government support. Art forms as diverse as women's needlework, pottery, and bell casting have given Korea a prominent position in world cultural history.

HIGHLIGHTS OF THE THREE KINGDOMS ERA

Korea's oldest existing works of art come from the fourth century's Three Kingdoms era. The first paintings, most of which were murals in cave tombs, were inspired by similar works in neighboring Manchuria. They were made near Pyongyang in what was Koguryo; some tomb paintings show men engaged in what appears to be an early form of martial arts. From Paekche came complex and colorful picture tiles and jade jewelry. The kingdom of Shilla left behind fine gold and jade jewelry, as well.

In the Shilla and Koryo eras Buddhism was the driving cultural force, especially in the areas of sculpture and architecture, of which many examples still survive. Korean architecture was influenced by four design elements: religion, natural surroundings and landscape, availability of materials, and a preference for simple lines. Splendid artwork filled Buddhist temples, and stone sculpture dedicated to Buddha in the grotto attached to the Pulguk Temple in Kyongju has been called the finest in Asia. The oldest existing observatory in Asia, made from stone and shaped like a bottle, was also built at Pulguk.

Author David Steinberg discusses some of the highlights of the early years of Buddhism in the Shilla kingdom. For example, "bronze construction was exceptional," he reports, citing a bell dating from the year 771 that is eleven feet high and more than seven feet in diameter. Buddhist monks were highly creative in the use of natural features to enhance their temples and monastery gardens. At one Buddhist monument, Steinberg reports, the statue of the Buddha was positioned

This astronomical observatory was built in the seventh century in Kyongju, the capital of Shilla. It is the oldest existing observatory in Asia.

so that the sun's first rays would "strike the Buddha's fore-head, creating a halo effect."[9] And gardens were crisscrossed by streams, whose flowing water carried miniature boats bearing cups of wine to courtiers, who often came to the peaceful temple gardens to write poetry.

One of history's most significant contributions to Buddhism was produced in the Koryo era: the *Tripitaka Koreana*, or *Scriptures of the Great Deeds*. It was a literary monument, printed from more than eighty thousand woodblocks engraved with the teachings and life story of the Buddha. Today, the *Tripitaka Koreana* is housed in a temple near Taegu.

EXQUISITE CELADON POTTERY OF THE KORYO

During the Koryo period the Academy of Painting was established, and Chinese influence showed itself in the selection of subjects painted: flowers, animals or birds, or landscapes. Perhaps the most famous art of Korea is its striking celadon pottery, which also was a product of the Koryo period. Though the artisans who produced it were among the lowest social class, today Korean celadon pottery is considered exquisitely beautiful. Korean celadon was glazed in a range of blues, greens, and grays at very high temperatures; the vessels can be quite plain or decorated with black and white natural objects such as flowers, cranes, or clouds. The Korean artisans who created it were inspired by and then surpassed Chinese pottery around the tenth century. Highly prized and valuable today, modern artisans try to reproduce it.

 ### TAOISM: ITS ANCIENT SYMBOL IS EVERYWHERE IN SOUTH KOREA

Taoism is another set of beliefs that came to Korea from China, most likely during the seventh century; it was especially well received in Shilla. Taoism stresses virtues such as simplicity, selflessness, and self-control to achieve health and overall well-being. Though it did not take root as a lasting religious group, examples of its influence are still very noticeable in Korea, such as the yin-yang symbol, representing harmony in opposites, applied to objects from the South Korean flag to coffee mugs. Divinators are sometimes consulted in making important decisions about life (such as marriage), another holdover from Taoism that still exists in Korea.

A celadon ceramic bottle from the Koryo period. The first two hundred years of the Koryo dynasty, which began in 935, saw a proliferation of art, including the famous celadon pottery.

In the Choson era, Korean artists moved further from Chinese influence and developed increasingly individual styles, which in turn influenced Japanese painting. One famous Korean painting from this era is *A Dream Visit to Peach Blossom Land.* The artist, with heavy shading and thick vertical forms, depicted strong and powerful mountains; nestled among them is a soft, horizontally arranged grove of trees, resting

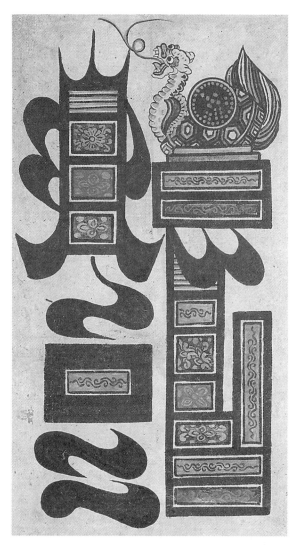

Korean calligraphy was a highly respected art form often practiced by Confucianists.

like a cloud in the jagged mountain peaks. Later, just as European artists moved away from classical subjects and began to paint more ordinary people and scenes, so did Korean artists who, in the seventeenth and eighteenth centuries, focused more on genre painting, or scenes of everyday life. Confucianism had its impact on art, too, mostly in the form of solemn portraits of Confucianist leaders, such as scholars or statesmen.

CALLIGRAPHY: THE MARK OF A GOOD CONFUCIANIST

Another art form in the Far East is calligraphy, or, simply, writing. But the art is anything but simple: "A calligraphic work would be hung on a wall like a painting and admired in the same way, each stroke being praised for its own attributes, the ink for its tone, and the whole composition for its strength [and] individuality," as *A Handbook of Korea* explains. The Korean alphabet called *han-gul* is derived from Chinese calligraphy, "in which each character is composed of a number of differently shaped strokes within an imaginary square," and has a different meaning.[10] A calligrapher needs four tools: ink, a brush, an ink stone, and good paper or silk. Skill in calligraphy was considered a sign of an accomplished Confucianist.

KOREAN MUSEUMS: KEEPERS OF CULTURE

South Korea has eight nationally sponsored museums whose collections contain a variety of artwork, from the art owned by royal families, to folk and ancient art, to modern works in many media. Three of those museums are located in Seoul and the others are in major cities that once served as capitals of ancient kingdoms. In addition, several cities and regions support their own museums, as do private collectors. For example, Chejudo has a museum devoted to the unique culture and natural history of the island, while Pusan boasts a museum of relics discovered at the sites of ancient burial tombs and mounds made from shells. The relatively new Seoul Arts Center includes the Seoul Opera House, Concert Hall, Calligraphy Hall, Arts Gallery, Arts Library, and Cultural Theme Park.

THE VALUE OF POETRY

Poetry was quite important in the old dynasties of Korea. A man's ability to compose a poem was considered a sign of how well he could serve his country, and how well educated he was. Scholars from China, in fact, once called Korea "the land of scholars and gentlemen."[11] Poetry was personal and spontaneous, often coming from individual experience, but was considered most effective if it spoke of something universal

HAN-GUL

King Sejong, the fourth monarch of Korea's Yi dynasty, has been called the Leonardo da Vinci of Korea. His rule in the 1400s was long, and marked by a variety of scientific and cultural accomplishments. The one for which he is most revered was his development of a Korean alphabet, called *han-gul*. In previous centuries, Koreans used Chinese script, even though orally the two languages are quite different. Chinese script is complex, and required much education for Korean scholars to master. The common working Korean had little chance or opportunity of learning it. Sejong wanted written communication to be possible throughout Korean society.

He assigned a group of scholars to study other written languages for ideas on how the Korean language might be put in writing. Sejong spent several years working on an alphabet; he and his scholarly assistants came up with a system in which each vowel sound has its own character, as does each consonant. So, for example, the character for *k* is combined with the character for the *ah* sound, and it makes the syllable sounding like *kah*. The alphabet created by Sejong had fourteen consonants and eleven vowels, and remains the same today, except that one vowel has been dropped. It has been called one of the most perfect writing systems ever created.

or addressed issues beyond the poet's own experience. Nature also played an important role in poetry, as shown in the following excerpt from a sixteenth-century poem, in which the poet uses a tree to symbolize what happens to a person who no longer enjoys political clout or favor:

> The tree is diseased;
>   no one rests in its pavilion.
> When it stood tall and verdant,
>   no one passed it by.
> But the leaves have fallen,
>   the boughs are broken;
>   not even birds perch there now.[12]

In some places in Korea poetry is actually a *part* of nature, inscribed into rocks next to waterfalls or in mountain passes, or at scenic spots, and even the outdoor pillars of a home. Poetry still is an important form of art in South Korea today. Poets have a wide variety of literary magazines in which to publish their work, and substantial prizes for which to compete.

KOREAN LITERATURE

Korean writers were recording history and important religious events as early as the sixth century, when a scholar devised a system of translating the Korean language into Chinese characters. Korean literature traces its beginning to the sixteenth century with *The Story of Hong Kil-tong*, the fictionalized story of the man who, like Robin Hood, robbed from the rich and gave to the poor. It pointed out the greed of nobles and public officials, and suggested that the rigid class system should be abolished. Other classic Korean works feature stories about the conflicts that sometimes occurred between Buddhist and Confucian philosophies (*The Nine Cloud Dream*), a love story that has been turned into folk opera (*The Story of Ch'unhyang*), and historical fiction (*The Tale of Queen Inhyon*).

Mujong (*The Heartless*), written by Yi Kwangsu and published in 1917, has become a modern classic on the subject of Korean-style arranged marriages versus marrying for love. Considered a prominent author of the twentieth century, Yi is also known for his works *Sarang* (*The Love*) and *Huk* (*The Soil*). Other modern classics include *Peace Under Heaven*, published in the 1930s, which looks at Korean life under Japanese domination; *The Poetry of John* is a product of postwar Korea, published in 1955, and expresses the frustration of living in a country where basic human rights are denied by a totalitarian government. Books written by Kang Younghill, such as *East Goes West*, illustrate the influence of English literature upon Korea.

SOUTH KOREAN MUSIC: STATELY OR LIVELY

Perhaps no other art form shows the stamp of Western culture in South Korea as much as music. "Typical" Korean music in the twentieth century can be anything from American pop music, to classical music from Europe, to South Korea's own mix of classical and folk music as well as romantic ballads.

While Western classical music is much admired and played by South Korean orchestras, the country's native music flourishes, as well. Traditional Korean music, with its five-note scale, is quite different from Western music, and its rhythms are complex. In general, there are two categories of Korean music: Chong'ak, which was formal and performed at a slow and stately pace at primarily royal and aristrocratic banquets or ceremonies; and its opposite, Korean folk music, which has an intensely fast rhythm and pace. Chong'ak can still be heard at the royal ancestral shrine and, in ceremonies honoring Confucius, at the University of Sonngyungwan.

Within the two categories of Chong'ak and folk music fall several types of vocal songs: Kagok, which are long, lyric songs; Sijo, which are shorter songs; Ch'angguk, a type of musical drama inspired by Chinese opera; P'ansori and Kasa, which are storytelling songs; and Pomp'ae, which are Buddhist chants.

In a Korean orchestra, instruments are arranged by the material from which they are made, such as metal, clay, stone, wood, silk, and other natural materials. A total of forty-five stringed instruments, gongs, flutes, and drums have been identified. One popular instrument is the *kayagum*, a long zither with twelve silk strings and twelve movable bridges. There are entire orchestras made up of just the *kayagum*, which the musicians play sitting on the floor. Another native Korean instrument is the *changgo*, a large hourglass-shaped drum played to accompany folk dancers.

Kyung-Wha Chung on violin and her sister Myung-Wha Chung on cello perform in London, England.

SOUTH KOREANS EXCEL IN WESTERN CLASSICAL MUSIC

It was Christian missionaries from Europe who introduced Korea to Western classical music, and today South Korea has several orchestras. Some of the world's leading classical musicians are from South Korea: Kyung-Wha Chung, a violinist who has performed internationally since 1968; violinists Dong Suk Kang and Yong Uck Kim; and pianists Kun Woo Paik and Ju Hee Suh. Seoul also hosts the National Opera Company and National Chorus.

Korean Isang Yun is a renowned composer in the European tradition whose artistic life often became entangled with politics. Born in Japanese-occupied Korea in 1917, he was educated in Japan but imprisoned by the Japanese in the 1940s. After the Korean War he taught at Seoul University until he began studying and traveling abroad in the 1950s. When he returned to South Korea ten years later, he was imprisoned for being a Communist; upon his release, he immigrated to Germany where, in spite of an offer of amnesty from the South Korean government, he remains.

TRADITIONAL KOREAN DANCE: ELEGANT OR EXCITING

Korean dance can be colorful and energetic, much like Korea itself. Like its music, Korean dance often was an important part of religious ceremonies and rituals, whether performed during a Buddhist ceremony or by farmers who danced to encourage a good harvest by pleasing the helpful spirits, or to chase away evil ones.

Dance also was important entertainment at the royal court. For example, each year on the first Sunday of May, a ceremony honoring the spirits of twenty kings and queens from the Choson dynasty is performed. This type of dance, a court dance, is slow and gracious. Women dancers wear traditional costumes of brightly colored silk skirts and tunics and elaborately ornamental headpieces. Court dancers strove for grace and control in their slow movements as they performed dances such as "Beautiful People Picking Peonies" or the "Crane Dance."

Folk dancing originated among the farmers, who danced for several days at planting or harvest festivals, or just during a rest period amid a regular day's work. These dances are especially energetic and athletic, performed by men and women to music by traditional folk percussion bands. Some traditional dances are performed with masks, and act out stories. Small towns in the country still play host to a variety of dance festivals, and within Seoul itself is a re-creation of a

A street performance of the traditional "Crane Dance" in Seoul. This dance was originally performed for ceremonies at the royal court.

2023-06-01

 MASKED DANCES AS A FORM OF PROTEST

In the Choson dynasty, where Seoul was the capital city, most of the highest-ranking *yangban* were from the southern half of the Korean peninsula, while people from the north often were looked down upon. One creative way the northerners voiced their protests about the *yangban* system was through the masked dance. The disguised dancers addressed a variety of issues through their performances, such as the increasing corruption of Buddhism, or the follies of the *yangban* and their lifestyle, which often seemed lacking in moral values.

Masked dancing was still popular as the twentieth century began, but might have been lost after the Korean War if not for some older dancers who taught their art to younger Koreans. One masked dance company based in Seoul, called Eunyul Talch'um, has been designated as a national cultural treasure and many of its dancers as national living treasures by the South Korean government for their preservation of the dance form.

country village where visitors can see what rural life was like for earlier generations of Koreans.

One striking Korean dance is the fan dance, or the *buchae chum*, which is described in *Faces* magazine. Each dancer holds a fan, which

> serve as an extension of the dancers' arms. The dancers move in a circular pattern, swaying to the music. Sometimes they come together in pairs, their large feather-edged fans fluttering like butterflies. Sometimes a wave ripples around the circle.

The dance comes to an end when the fans are slowly lifted and dropped, "creating the illusion of a flower opening and closing."[13]

Aspring artists, musicians, singers, and dancers of all varieties can receive training at several universities in South Korea, the newest of which is the Korean National University of Arts, established in 1993.

At Home and at School

Tough and independent, serious and patriotic, generous and warmhearted; these are some of the descriptions of South Koreans frequently given by visitors to that country. One thing the South Koreans are not is boring. Writer Don Oberdorfer uses two high-powered comparisons when he says that Korean people are "about as subtle as *kimchi*, the fiery pepper-and-garlic concoction that is their national dish, and as timid as a *tae kwon do* (Korean karate) chop."[14]

The country appears ultramodern with skyscrapers and traffic-clogged superhighways. Multifloor office and apartment buildings cast their shadows over centuries-old architecture. But the orderly, reverent Confucian approach to life, a holdover from dynasties long gone, still has much effect on the way South Koreans live, whether they practice Buddhism, Christianity, or no religion at all. Under their modern-style suits, dresses, or blue jeans are people who remain very much influenced by their Confucian heritage.

THE LONG-LASTING EFFECTS OF CONFUCIANISM

The Confucian sense of authority and duty is very strong in Korean society, whether between parent and child (including adult children and their parents), children and their teacher, or employees and employers. Even younger siblings must call their older sisters or brothers by a special term, rather than their name: *Onni*, for older sister, or *Obha*, for older brother. Not surprisingly, South Korea is considered Asia's most Confucian country. Its people in general put in long workdays, an indication of their competitive and disciplined approach to life. But at the same time they are a feisty, spirited people who can only be pushed so far: Students demonstrating against unfair government policies have been a part of the Korean culture for centuries, too.

Reverence for ancestors is shown several times each year in Confucian rituals established hundreds of years ago, and being elderly still wins one some degree of automatic respect. Though Confucianism's strict lines of social rank no longer exist, some claim that family connections still are important in gaining entry into universities or a career. Korea remains a patriarchal society, where men hold more authority, and women earn considerably less than men.

All people born in South Korea are listed on their father's family register; a woman remains on her father's register even when she marries. She keeps her family surname, though

A DUTIFUL DAUGHTER

Duty first, self last; that kind of attitude is the backbone of Confucianism, and South Korean parents and schools strive to instill it in their children. The old but still popular folktale about Shim Chung is an attempt to show children that dutiful behavior reaps many rewards.

Shim Chung and her blind father were poor, but she took good care of him. The father fell into a river one day, and was saved by a Buddhist monk, who told the blind man that he could regain his eyesight if he brought three hundred bags of rice to the temple. But Shim Chung's father had barely enough rice for himself and his daughter.

When Shim Chung heard of the monk's offer, she wanted more than anything to help her father regain his sight. Shortly after, some sailors arrived in the town, and wanted to sail to China. But they were afraid to do so without making a human sacrifice to the sea dragon to ensure a safe voyage. Shim Chung heard about this, and offered herself as the sacrifice, if the sailors would take three hundred bags of rice to the temple. They agreed.

Shim Chung sailed off with the sailors, and when a wild storm tossed the boat about, she jumped into the sea as she called out to her father. Shim Chung did not drown, but was taken to the Sea King, who wanted her for his own daughter. Shim Chung could not stay, though, because she thought only of her father. She was taken back up to the sea's surface within a lotus flower; sailors found the flower and took it to the king. When Shim Chung came out of the flower, the king fell in love with her, and they married. She lived a royal life in the palace where she and her new husband were joined by her father, who did indeed regain his eyesight. A dutiful beginning made for a happy ending!

once she has children she is more likely to be called "mother of so-and-so" than her own name. Traditionally, a mother's parents are considered less important family members than the father's parents. The extended family, or clan, once was very tightly knit. It remains an important factor in Korean life; for example, most city dwellers are only one or two generations removed from a small rural village, and will likely return to that village at least twice each year to visit the graves of ancestors. But for more and more families, that bond has loosened as they have relocated. One sign of that trend in recent years is the high rate of infants placed in orphanages. Most of these babies would have been cared for within the extended family in an earlier era.

The three most common surnames, or family names, in Korea are Kim, Lee, and Park, which together make up about 40 percent of the population; altogether, there are only about 250 surnames among all Koreans. As among other Asians, the Korean family name precedes the given name, though one exception was Syngman Rhee, as he became known in the West (in Korea, he was still Rhee Syngman).

Until very recently, it was illegal for men and women to marry if they shared the same family name and if their family was from the same region. That eliminated a lot of marriage possibilities for the 3.7 million Kims from Kimhae, for example, or the 2.7 million Parks from Miryang, or the almost 2.4 million Lees from Chonju. The national government finally bowed to public pressure to do away with that law, but the *Christian Science Monitor* reports that as recently as 1997, Confucian scholars were warning that the new law would lead "toward immorality and chaos."[15]

TRADITIONAL HOMES GIVE WAY TO HIGH-RISE APARTMENTS

Though South Koreans still are influenced by the past, the homes they live in have undergone many changes. The traditional Korean house, dating from the Choson era, is a rectangular thatched-roof structure of two rooms, a kitchen and a multipurpose room. Originally, walls were made of clay over wood frames. Sliding doors and windows made from heavy paper actually were quite effective in keeping out cold air. A Korean home, grand or small, used a unique form of heating called *ondol*, in which the warmth from the kitchen fire was spread through flues under the floor throughout the home.

Wealthier families' homes comprised several buildings enclosed by a wall with a gate. Men's and women's quarters were separate (since extended families usually shared a home), as well as servants' quarters, guest rooms, and a family shrine. A natural setting was considered ideal for any home, disrupting nature as little as possible. Houses often faced south, with mountains to the back and sides.

Furniture was used sparingly. Mattresses were rolled up and stored when not in use, and floor cushions served for sitting. Short-legged tables were pulled out when needed. Thus the extra room in a smaller house could be used as a living or dining room, or for sleeping. Even today, some families stick to the traditional way of keeping furniture out of sight as much as possible, while others "furnish" their homes in the Western sense with beds and dining tables kept in their places at all times. One Korean tradition that has not changed is that of taking off shoes upon entering a home.

A traditional Korean home was a thatched-roof dwelling usually consisting of two rooms. The homes of wealthy Korean families could include several buildings.

The traditional single-family homes of the Choson era are becoming scarce, as land becomes more scarce. A housing shortage in South Korea has meant that the historic thatched-roof cottages once found throughout the countryside are making way for newer housing. Most Koreans live in increasingly crowded cities today, and for them high-rise apartment buildings, with just one family per apartment, are the norm.

TRADITIONAL CLOTHING IN THE MODERN AGE

Though for practical reasons Koreans are giving up the traditional form of housing, the old style of Korean clothing, called *hanbok*, still is worn for special occasions. *Hanbok* evolved over many centuries, and was influenced by Chinese and Mongolian clothing styles. Men's *hanbok* consists of a short

Apartment buildings, such as these in Seoul, are the typical homes for the majority of South Koreans today.

loose-fitting jacket with wide sleeves, called a *chigori*, and is fastened with a large button or jewel-stone through a loop. A *chigori* is worn over baggy pants that are tied at the waist and ankles. A woman's short blouse, also called a *chigori*, crosses over in front and is tied at the side with ribbons. It is worn over a long, wraparound skirt.

Clothing was loose to accommodate several layers of underclothing in winter, which often substituted for wearing a coat. The traditional clothing that some Korean people still wear on special holidays such as *Sol*, or New Year's Day, dates back to the Choson era. "The body was as fully covered as much as possible, reflecting the Confucian sense of decency,"[16] writes Elizabeth Lee in *The Koreans*. Korea's upper classes wore brightly colored silk clothing, while commoners tended to wear cotton in muted colors. Men and women wore hats indoors and out, and hat styles could also indicate social rank. Today, some younger Korean men are showing a renewed interest in wearing *hanbok*. But generally, especially in the large cities, Western-style clothing prevails.

The most elaborate hanbok *was made of brilliantly colored silk. Traditional Korean clothing is still worn for special occasions.*

CELEBRATING LIFE'S MILESTONES

A variety of special celebrations mark a Korean's life, the first occurring when a baby is one hundred days old. Before the era of modern medicine, infant mortality was high all over the world, and so Koreans celebrated the one-hundred-day milestone as a special achievement. Though far fewer babies die today in infancy, it still is an important celebration. A feast is held for family and friends, and, most importantly, one hundred rice cakes are distributed throughout the neighborhood to symbolically assure the child of a long, prosperous life.

The highlight of the child's first birthday, or *tol*, is the baby's "prediction" of his or her future. Wearing brightly colored traditional clothing, the toddler is seated before a table laden with objects representing a variety of professions. For example, if the baby picks up food such as a cake, it symbolizes his or her becoming a government worker someday, or a calligraphy brush symbolizes a future scholar. If rice or money is picked up, the toddler might grow up to be wealthy.

The next important birthday is *hwan-gap* at age sixty, again considered important because in earlier times few people lived that long, and because, by that age, a person has lived through a complete cycle of the zodiac constellations.

The sixty-year-old is honored by his or her children with a grand celebration attended by family and friends; in another ten years the seventieth birthday, called *kohi* (meaning "old and rare"), is the occasion for a similarly festive celebration.

Weddings in Korea can vary in ceremony from quite traditional Korean to a Western-style wedding in a church or rented hall. In Korea's earlier days, the bride and groom did not meet until their wedding day, which had been arranged by their parents. In fact, from about the age of seven, males and females were kept apart. Even today, some parents suggest marriage partners for their sons and daughters, but the prospective bride and groom are not bound by the parents' choices.

In a traditional wedding, the bride and groom stand face to face, separated by a table bearing symbols of a happy marriage: lighted candles, a pair of carved ducks, skeins of thread in blue and red. Wedding rituals include deep bows to each other and the guests, a ceremonial hand washing, and exchanging a cup of wine. Though this traditional wedding service has slipped from common practice, it is being revived by more couples.

Romantic love is not always a key ingredient in a wedding in Korea, even today. One young Korean man told an American newspaper reporter that "Most people don't marry for love. They marry for business or political reasons." Another Korean man, a Confucian scholar, explained to the same journalist that marriage in Korea is important not just for individuals, but for an entire family: "Here, you get married for everyone's happiness."[17] Historically, divorce has been very rare in Korea: As late as the mid-1980s, less than .5 percent of the population was divorced, though that figure has gradually increased.

SOL: A MUCH-ANTICIPATED HOLIDAY

Among the variety of annual holidays celebrated by South Korean families, the most festive is *Sol,* the new year. Koreans today use the Gregorian calendar that Western countries follow, and the new year officially begins on January 1. But the big celebration is saved for the traditional New Year's Day, or the first day of the first month in a lunar calendar, which usually comes in February. It is actually a holiday season, lasting about two weeks, and for some of its events the entire family comes together. New clothes in the traditional styles are worn, a feast is prepared, and in many households rituals are performed to honor ancestors.

One such ritual takes place either at the family memorial tomb or in a room in which a memorial tablet or plaque is kept. A table nearby has been set full of specially prepared dishes. First, each family member takes a turn bowing twice before the ancestral tablet, which represents four generations of that family. Then, they enjoy the feast awaiting them at the table, which includes vegetable and meat dishes as well as rice cakes and wine.

Sabae is another ritual of respect performed for *Sol* when the family gathers: While facing older family members, the younger ones, while on their knees, bow down until their foreheads touch the floor. Then the older relatives present

LIFE AT SEA

The sea plays a great part in Korean life: it brings the monsoon rains each summer, and seafood is an important commodity, both for exporting and for the Korean diet. Another part of sea life is the culture of the islands scattered throughout South Korea's surrounding three seas. More than a hundred of them are inhabited, and a pair are especially famous. Chejudo has become a popular tourist destination, and Chindo might be best known for its rare breed of dog, also called the Chindo, which may not be taken off of the island.

In the 1980s, journalist and author Russell Warren Howe visited the South Korean island Kagodo, a thirty-hour boat ride from the southwest mainland, and wrote about it in his book *The Koreans*. Islanders there fish for anchovies at night, or other fish depending on the season, and farm seaweed. Barley is grown on the island instead of rice, and was the staple grain.

The few hundred families living on the island were, not surprisingly, quite isolated, and had fewer than twenty surnames among them. Marriages often were arranged when future brides and grooms were still children, and performed later if their horoscopes showed them to be compatible (a common step before marriage on the mainland, as well). Life on the island is quite independent of mainland government or police, and village elders serve as the island's authority figures. Young men who never do military service live out their days unaware of what the rest of their country is like.

them with small gifts, such as money or candy. Afterward, the children might visit other relatives or neighbors or even their teachers for more performances of *sabae*.

Special games are played during the new year season, like *yut*, a board game. A favorite among girls is Korean-style see-sawing. Two girls stand on either end of the see-saw board gradually increasing the height of their jumps until each girl can send the other flying up into the air. Since each girl must land on her feet at her end of the board, the activity requires skill and practice. This version of see-sawing is thought to date back to Confucian times: It allowed girls to catch a quick glimpse of the world outside the wall around their home, which they were not allowed to go beyond.

Kite flying is another pastime associated with *Sol*, but played more like a competitive sport. Kite strings are dabbed with glue, to which glass powder is stuck, making the string quite sharp. Kite flyers try to keep their kites in the air, while cutting the strings of their "opponents."

The see-saw game played by Korean girls dates back to times when unmarried women were confined to the walled yards of their houses. The jump allowed them a brief glimpse of the outside world.

GIVING THANKS

Ch'usok is another holiday, held at the end of the harvest season in fall and similar to America's Thanksgiving. Thanks are given for the harvest, and the family's feast will include special rice cakes, called *songpyon*, made from newly harvested grain. Family members will leave *songpyon* and other kinds of food at the family tomb when they visit it to honor their ancestors.

The Korean traditional diet makes much use of grains and vegetables, and less use of meat and fat. Two staples served at just about every Korean meal are rice and kimchi. The mild-tasting but filling rice complements the tangy kimchi, which is a spicy, pickled vegetable, usually cabbage. One finds kimchi everywhere in Korea, in homes and at restaurants; even school cafeterias serve it daily. Fall used to be kimchi season, when women would shred and soak dozens of heads of cabbage in liquid seasoning, and leave it to ferment in clay jars placed underground, where the temperature was cooler. Since vegetables are today available year-round, kimchi can be made anytime and kept stored in the refriger- ator, but the brown clay jars are still seen in every home.

SCHOOLS: A KOREAN PRIORITY

Education has always been important to Koreans, thanks to Confucian ideals. Commoners had little access to schooling, but that has changed dramatically in recent generations. "Even in the period of extreme poverty following the Korean War, primary schools dotted the Korean rural landscape,"[18] said David Steinberg. Today, the rate of literacy among South Koreans is almost 100 percent.

High school is serious business for Korean teenagers. School begins early in the morning and students are in classes for about eight hours. Then, they spend several more hours in study, perhaps until midnight or later. Altogether, they study twenty-seven subjects in three years of high school, which leads to an all-important multiple-choice examina- tion that determines which university they will attend. Pres- sure on students to get high scores on the exam, both from their schoolteachers and their families, is intense.

Parents spend thousands of dollars each year on private tu- toring for each of their children with the hope that they will be able to attend the best universities, which parents believe will make their children more successful later in life. Study hard now, Korean parents tell their teenagers in high school, and you will have time for fun in college. But over the years the number of high school students taking the exam has increased at a faster rate than the number of openings at the universities, which adds to the pressure students feel at test time.

UNIVERSITY ENTRANCE EXAMS

Just how important is the exam that South Ko- rean students take at the end of their high school years? On test day in Seoul in 1997, businesses started an hour late so students could have the normally busy streets to themselves while getting to school; during the test's listening comprehen- sion section, no airplanes landed or took off at the airport; the 175 teachers who wrote the test were kept in a hotel for a month while they worked on it, their windows covered over with paper and barbed-wire fences erected around the hotel.

Korean society values learning, as these eager young schoolchildren can attest. South Korea's focus on education has resulted in a literacy rate of nearly 100 percent.

In 1992 there were more than 2 million students in just under two thousand high schools; the rigorous, or demanding, schooling that South Korean teenagers receive was designed in the 1960s, when the country itself was working hard to improve living conditions for its people. In many ways, that goal has been achieved; most of the people of South Korea live well above the level of poverty that can plague other countries generation after generation.

But some South Korean educators and business leaders began questioning whether education in their country needs to be reexamined, arguing that cramming so many subjects and hours of study into three years in order to do well on a multiple-choice test will not necessarily teach a teenager such important skills as problem solving or thinking creatively. To address this concern, former South Korean president Kim Young Sam formed a committee to look at ways of reorganizing Korean high schools, so that future leaders of the country can meet head-on some of the complex economic and social issues that South Korea faces today and expects to face in the future.

THE ECONOMY
AND SOUTH-NORTH
RELATIONS

Resiliency and patriotism, it has been noted, are key characteristics of the Korean personality. Those qualities are behind perhaps the greatest story to have emerged from modern-day South Korea: its rise from an isolated, wartorn land of peasant farmers to a vibrant, bustling showplace of high technology. This transformation was accomplished within two generations and with few natural resources at hand.

By the late 1980s, Korea was one of the top trading countries in the world, filling America's and other markets with automobiles and a variety of electrical appliances. Factories had difficulty hiring enough workers, and this labor shortage caused workers' salaries to rise. Contributing to the high national average wage is the fifty- to sixty-hour Korean workweek, one of the longest in the industrialized world.

SOUTH KOREAN OPTIMISM UNDER ECONOMIC HARDSHIP

But ten years later, the economy in South Korea gave the world a scare: Many of its largest companies were on the verge of bankruptcy, deep in debt to foreign lenders. In turn South Koreans felt it their patriotic duty to shun foreign products. The Korean currency, called the won, took a sharp dive in value. Japan was going though a similar economic crisis, and such problems in a global economy have worldwide effects. South Korean businesses received international loans to help meet debt obligations, but in exchange they were required to change the way they operate, as well as make their businesses smaller. No longer feeling the pinch of labor shortages, South Korean companies in the late 1990s were for the first time having to lay off workers.

As he took office in the winter of 1998, Korean president Kim Dae Jung called his country's financial problems "the most serious national crisis since the Korean War."[19] But he also has expressed optimism that South Korea not only will conquer its economic woes, but will come out even stronger. Ranked as the eleventh-largest economy in the world, South Korea could reach the fifth position, Kim predicted.

In the meantime, many South Koreans suffer from unemployment, but Kim's optimism can be heard among the

ECONOMIC MODEL?

Following the Korean War, South Korea had one of the lowest per capita incomes, or the average amount of money made by its citizens, in the world. Financial and material aid, both from the government and private citizens of the United States, prevented many in South Korea from starving. Today, countries trying to improve their own economics study South Korea as a model. Once a poor country itself, within thirty years it became the eleventh-largest economy in the world. Giving business lots of help, having a population of hard workers, but holding back on democracy until the country was more settled seemed to be the key to the economic success of South Korean president Park Chung Hee in the 1960s and '70s.

But one theory about South Korea suggests there were plenty of other factors behind the country's success that would be almost impossible to duplicate elsewhere.

To begin with, the Japanese occupation and then the Korean War made the old social system of *yangban* and commoners useless. Following those catastrophes, anyone willing to work hard could find economic success. Additionally, the United States gave Seoul billions of dollars in the twenty years following South Korea's liberation from Japan, helping industry get started. The American military stationed there also pumped money into the economy.

Impoverished by events in their recent history, the Koreans had no qualms about taking risks, which paid off in the 1970s and '80s. For example, Park Chung Hee wanted to build steel mills, an expensive investment that U.S. advisers warned against. But when the U.S. military needed equipment for the Vietnam War, South Korea's steel mills provided much of it. Later, the steel industry exported a variety of products, including cars, to the United States and elsewhere.

South Korea can point to its determination, hard work, and planning as the factors in its economic success of the 1980s and '90s. But much of that success also is due to unique circumstances of history.

people of Seoul, as well. One example is forty-eight-year-old Pae Jong Min, who sells dried squid in a street market; like Kim, he did not expect the financial crisis to last long. "Korean people are very diligent," he told a newspaper reporter as 1997 came to a close. "People have been spending too much. Now they will cut back. I think in a couple of years, things will get better."[20]

REUNIFICATION: WHEN, NOT IF

And, like other South Koreans, Pae likes to say that North and South Korea will be reunited within a decade.

One question mark hovering above South Korea's shaky economy is the growing assumption that North Korea will collapse in the near future, its government no longer able to provide a living or services for its people. "Without question, North Korea will need roads and manufacturing equipment, billions of dollars in new ports, a telephone system

 ## LAYOFFS: SOMETHING NEW FOR SOUTH KOREANS

As the year 1998 progressed, many South Koreans were making difficult adjustments: layoffs were on the increase, doubling the unemployment rate and sending crime and suicide rates up, as well.

Employees in South Korea's booming economy were used to thinking that their jobs would last as long as they could work. But as South Korean big business tries to solve its debt problems by downsizing, tens of thousands of workers have been let go. More than twice as many small business owners declared bankruptcy in 1998 as in 1997. At the same time, the cost of necessities such as food and fuel has gone up.

Many of South Korea's jobless have responded to their plight in a way that astonishes longtime Korea-watchers, and doubtless themselves: They are turning to petty crime. Manhole covers stolen from city streets have turned up for sale at metal recycling plants. Large trucks parked on the streets have their gas tanks siphoned empty during the night. Middle-aged housewives are caught shoplifting at grocery stores. Some desperate citizens are trying their hands at burglary or breaking and entering. Most of the lawbreakers are caught, however, because they are not very good at these illegal pursuits.

that works and a safety net for a population that periodically veers toward starvation,"[21] according to a report in the *New York Times*.

As different as the two countries are in their government and politics, unification of Korea has been a fairly steady topic of discussion between North and South Korea since 1971. Ten million families are separated by the Demilitarized Zone; photographs of somber-faced Koreans holding up signs with names of loved ones living across the border, so that television cameras can broadcast their messages, illustrate what an emotional issue separation has been.

"MILLIONS OF SAD STORIES"

"Many members of separated families have grown old and are passing away. We must let those separated from their families in the South and the North meet and communicate with each other as soon as possible,"[22] declared Kim Dae Jung as he called for Korean reunification in his presidential inauguration speech in February 1998.

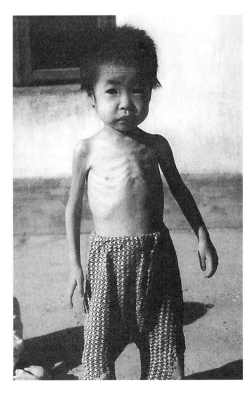

A malnourished young boy near Pyongyang is evidence of North Korea's bouts of food shortages.

But the simplest forms of communication between North and South Koreans are infrequent at best. There is neither mail nor telephone service between the two countries, much less diplomatic relations between their governments. In both South and North Korea it is against the law to listen to radio broadcasts coming from the other country.

Chun Sun Tae, a South Korean businessman who lives in California, predicted that if the fifty-year separation of North and South Korea ended, many of the estimated 10 million Koreans living away from their countries would immediately head home. Like him, many of them left North Korea during the Korean War, but still have family there. He left his home at age thirteen to look for his father, who had yet to return home from the war. Almost as soon as Chun left, his father returned home. But Chun was unable to cross back over the border at the 38th parallel. He eventually immigrated to America, never to see his father again. He was able to see his

mother and brothers after a thirty-year separation when a Los Angeles organization
arranged for a small number of Koreans to
visit families there. "In my hometown,
which was near the border, eighty percent
of families are separated. I am only one of
millions—millions of sad stories,"[23] he told
a newspaper reporter.

Showing the influences of Confucianism as well as the national despair over the
Korean separation, Kim Dae Jung said in
his inaugural speech that "I cannot but
feel boundless shame before our ancestors
who maintained one unified country for
more than 1,300 years,"[24] though he also
declared that the south would not tolerate
aggressive actions from the north.

*South Korean president
Kim Dae Jung advocates
reunification with
North Korea.*

COMMUNICATION STRUGGLES BETWEEN SOUTH AND NORTH

There was little discussion between the two Koreas following
the 1950s war and through the 1960s. Syngman Rhee sought
the presidency, not dialogue with the Communists to the
north. In the early 1970s, during the presidency of Park
Chung Hee, a series of meetings were held between representatives of both countries, and a telephone hotline installed between Seoul and Pyongyang seemed to represent
progress. But differing politics stalled the talks. Other meetings were held throughout the decade, without results.

Early in 1982 South Korean president Chun put forth a de-
tailed plan for unification calling for a council made up of
citizens from both sides who would together write a constitution for a reunited Korea. General elections throughout the
peninsula would be held to put a government in place. The
north, perhaps because it has only half the population of
South Korea, announced its rejection of the plan within a
few days.

In 1984 the north put forth a proposal of its own: It suggested a three-way discussion between North and South
Korea and the United States. It also wanted to sign new
treaties between the United States and North Korea that
would supercede the Korean War Armistice Agreement,
which had ended the war. North Korea's primary goal in

these negotiations was to see U.S. troops return home. The south counterproposed that the two Koreas schedule meetings to settle their differences, without involving the United States, but no meetings occurred.

Later that year, Chun proposed a joint economic venture between north and south. Things looked hopeful as North Korea sent relief packages to flood victims in South Korea, and agreed to a new series of meetings. The first meeting was fairly productive, with trade possibilities discussed and more proposals for family visit-exchanges, but a follow-up discussion was canceled after an incident at the DMZ in which soldiers from both sides died. North Korea canceled more scheduled discussions for early 1985 in protest of the "Team Spirit" exercises held each winter by the South Korean and American armies at the DMZ. The annual Team Spirit exercise, in which the two armies flex their military muscle in full view of the North Korean army, has always been an irritant to North Korea, and more meetings in future years would be canceled because of it.

 ## DEFECTORS FROM NORTH TO SOUTH KOREA

Those who defect, or escape, from Communist North Korea to capitalist South Korea may envision a better life for themselves, but they usually go through a difficult time of adjustment. One of the first things they notice is a language difference: South Koreans use some Chinese characters in their written language, as well as a variety of foreign words such as "shampoo." The fast pace and advanced technology of South Korea can seem overwhelming, and the unsophisticated North Koreans often are easy prey for con artists who swindle them of money they have been given by the South Korean government. They also feel grief and guilt for leaving loved ones behind.

By the mid-1990s, the South Korean government has had only a trickle of defectors: Fewer than eight hundred were living in South Korea at that point. Some defectors have been high-profile North Korean government officials. But with North Korea's mounting problems, the main one being the hunger of its people, the South Korean government is facing the possibility that thousands of needy North Koreans might overcome border guardposts to seek new lives in South Korea.

AFTER THIRTY YEARS, SOME REUNIONS

But something positive did come out of meetings later in 1985: "For the first time since the end of the Korean War, sizable numbers of private citizens crossed the Demilitarized Zone in both directions with official approval."[25] But such successes were occasional and unpredictable. In general, North Korea was more willing to talk reunification if the U.S. Army left the peninsula, while South Korea did not trust the north's declarations of good intentions.

By the 1990s, North Korea's economy was in shambles, and many of its people lived under worse conditions than their peasant ancestors had a century earlier. North Korea's former mentor, the Soviet Union, had disbanded, leaving Russia and the other independent states resulting from the breakup with big financial problems of their own. South Korean president Roh Tae Woo and North Korea's aging dictator Kim Il Sung first met in 1991, amid excited talk of exchanges in technology and economics and the possibility of more contacts between separated families. Continued discussions were making headway: Each country's prime minister agreed to form a committee that would implement plans to get rid of all nuclear arms in South Korea, as well as plans to begin a true economic partnership. By 1992 there had been hundreds of visits on either side of the DMZ by athletes, performing arts groups, and individuals seeking out family members. But in spite of the removal by the U.S. military of all of its nuclear warheads in South Korea, before long North Korea gave much of the world a scare when credible rumors surfaced indicating that the north was secretly planning to make a nuclear bomb.

A WAR SCARE

North Korea was refusing to cooperate with the international Nuclear Non-Proliferation Treaty, which was backed up by inspectors of the UN International Atomic Energy Agency. Representatives of the IAEA travel around the world to inspect nuclear facilities with a view to halting or slowing the manufacture of nuclear arms. Though North Korea had signed the nonproliferation treaty, its government turned IAEA inspectors away from one suspected nuclear plant. World attention became riveted on North Korea: Was it trying to manufacture an atomic bomb, and, if so, how would the weapon be used? The new president in South Korea, Kim Young Sam, whose mother had been killed by North Koreans in 1960, refused to negotiate the issue, and by 1994 citizens of Seoul were envisioning another war. They began hoarding emergency supplies of extra rice and candles, while the South Korean government stockpiled arms. Meanwhile, in the United States, the Pentagon developed a war plan for the Korean peninsula.

Former U.S. president Jimmy Carter, who had had success as a peace broker in other tense political situations, offered to travel to North Korea as a private citizen to see what might be done to convince North Korea to be more cooperative toward nuclear plant inspectors. The Clinton administration accepted his offer and, over the objections of South Korea's President Kim, Carter traveled to North Korea in June 1994.

Upon meeting with the elderly Kim Il Sung, Carter made a proposal to which Kim agreed: International inspectors would be allowed to remain in North Korea in exchange for a commitment from the United States to reestablish diplomatic talks begun earlier in the decade with North Korea. Kim also agreed to halt all processing of materials that could be used for nuclear weapons. Carter believed that North Korea would have gone to war if the United Nations had imposed economic sanctions against the north and at the same time the United States had increased its arms supply to the south. Carter arranged for the U.S. government to supply North Korea with heavy fuel oil for energy use, and both Korean presidents expressed willingness to start their own diplomatic discussions anew, now that the nuclear weapons crisis seemed resolved. But before the talks could be renewed, Kim Il Sung died.

Roh Tae Woo, South Korea's president from 1987 to 1993, negotiated with North Korea for possible economic partnerships and allowing separated families to reunite.

OPTIMISM FOR REUNIFICATION REMAINS HIGH

As of 1998 those talks still were on hold. Under the leadership
of Kim Il Sung's son Kim Jong Il, North Korea continued its pat-
tern of agreeing to talks and then canceling them when it was
clear that the United States would not be recalling its thirty-
seven thousand troops anytime soon. The newest President
Kim of North Korea, rarely appearing in public, remains a
mystery to outsiders, and no doubt to his own people. Meanwhile, the people of North Korea continued to make head-
lines as famine victims, and it is believed that North Korea
still works secretly to manufacture nuclear weapons.

Though unification talks remain at a standstill, to many
South Koreans it seems almost certain that unification will
happen. Joon-Sik Park is a South Korean native living in the
United States and a minister at a United Methodist Church
in Ohio. The subject of reuniting peacefully with North Korea
is a passionate one for South Koreans, Park says. "Most South
Koreans feel very strongly for it. We were, and we are, one
country, with one language and one culture."[26] He believes
that younger Koreans, who did not go through the bitter experience of the Korean War, feel especially compassionate
toward the suffering North Koreans, and are optimistic about
a unified Korea. That is particularly so today, Park said, since
the world has also witnessed the reunification of Germany

*While on patrol, armed
South Korean soldiers
at the Demilitarized
Zone look through a
fence to the north.
Relations between
North and South Korea
along the border have
remained tense.*

A NEW ERA FOR SOUTH KOREA

In its brief history, the fifty-year-old Republic of Korea has gone through dramatic changes. Most notable is that the rural "Hermit Kingdom" is now a world industrial leader. Equally important, political leaders have had to give some degree of political control to the Korean people. One clear example of that took place while Kim Young Sam was in office: Two former presidents, Chun Doo Hwan and Roh Tae Woo, were found guilty of offenses commited while they were in office. Chun's handling of the Kwangju uprising finally caught up to him, and both were found guilty of "conspiring" to take over the government when Chun passed on leadership to Roh. That they were put on trial was unusual in itself; when President Kim at first declined to imprison them, the volume of public protests led Kim to change his mind, and today the two former leaders are in prison.

and seen the people of Eastern Europe turn to democracy. Those major changes that occurred in Europe make the reunification of the two Koreas seem more possible than ever to South Koreans.

"WE ARE ONE PEOPLE"

In spite of their own country's financial problems, South Koreans are ready to embrace the impoverished northern Koreans. While the per capita income for South Koreans is more than $10,000 per year, for North Koreans it is less than $1,000. "I'm prepared to share the burden if our country is reunited," said a Seoul street vendor, forty-five-year-old Lee Soon Yi, who sells clothing from his wooden cart. "North Koreans are very diligent. They have a lot of natural resources underground. . . . After five or six years of hardships, it will make us stronger,"[27] Lee told a newspaper reporter.

At the other end of the economic scale is Hwang Young Key, a corporate executive in Seoul who also sees economic advantages to reunification. He points out that Korean businesses would have 20 million more hard workers, who will provide a larger market for new products.

But, mostly, reunification is an issue of the heart for South Koreans. Of course, it will happen, said a woman in Seoul. "It is very simple. We are one people."[28]

FACTS ABOUT SOUTH KOREA

SOUTH KOREA IS DIVIDED INTO NINE PROVINCES:

Cheju
Kangwŏn
Kyŏnggi
North Chŏlla
North Ch'ungch'ŏng
North Kyŏngsang
South Chŏlla
South Ch'ungch'ŏng
South Kyŏngsang

METROPOLITAN AREAS

In addition, there are six large metropolitan areas, called "special cities," that are governed like a province: Seoul, Pusan, Inch'on, Taegu, Kwangju, and Taejŏn

PRESIDENTS

Syngman Rhee, 1948–1960
Yun Po-sun, 1960–1961
Park Chung Hee, 1961–1979
Choi Kyu-hah, 1979
Chun Doo Hwan, 1979–1987
Roh Tae Woo, 1987–1993
Kim Young Sam, 1993–1997
Kim Dae Jung, 1997–

DEMOGRAPHY

Population - 45,482,291
Population density - 1,197 people/square mile
By gender - males: 50.4%; females: 49.6%
Population by age - 0–14 years old: 23%; 15–64 years old: 71%; 65 and older: 6%

Religion (as percentage of those declaring any religious affiliation) - Christianity: 48.6%; Buddhism: 47.4%; Confucianism: 3%; other (such as Shamanism): .2%

Major metropolitan areas and population - Seoul: 10.9 million; Pusan: 3.8 million; Taegu: 2.2 million; Inch'on: 2.1 million; Kwangju: 2 million; Taejŏn: 2 million

Native/foreign residents - South Korea has a homogenous population with no significant minorities, except for about 20,000 Chinese

Annual birthrate - 16.24 per 1,000 people

Annual death rate - 5.66 per 1,000 people

Annual marriage rate - 7 per 1,000 people

Life expectancy at birth - overall average: 73.26 years; males: 69.65 years; females: 77.3 years

LAND

Land area, square miles - 38,370

Land use - agriculture: 22%; forest, woodlands: 67%; meadows, pastures: 1%; other: 10%

Highest point - Mount Halla, on Chejudo, at 6,396 ft.

Largest island - Chejudo

NATIONAL ECONOMY

GDP (US$) - $476 billion (1997)

GDP growth rate - 6.2% (1997)

Currency - won; 964.5 won = $1 (1997)

Budget:
Revenue in US$ - $48.4 billion (1993)
Expenditures in US$ - $48.4 billion (1993)

Per capita income - $10,530 (1997)

Imports and major import sources - $146 billion: crude oil, machinery and transportation equipment, chemicals/chemical products, base metals; suppliers: Japan, United States, European Union, Middle East

Exports and major export destinations - $130 billion: manufactures, textiles, ships, automobiles, steel, computers, footwear; major markets: United States, Japan, ASEAN (Association of Southeast Asian Nations), European Union

NOTES

CHAPTER 2: THE EARLIEST KOREANS

1. Don Oberdorfer, *The Two Koreas: A Contemporary History.* Reading, MA: Addison-Wesley, 1997, p. 3.

2. *A Handbook of Korea.* 9th ed. Seoul: Korean Overseas Information Service, 1993, p. 135.

CHAPTER 3: CHOSON: A FIVE-HUNDRED-YEAR DYNASTY

3. *A Handbook of Korea*, p. 66.

4. David Steinberg, *The Republic of Korea: Economic Transformation and Social Change.* Boulder, CO: Westview Press, 1989, p. 34.

5. *A Handbook of Korea*, p. 86.

6. Quoted in Steinberg, *The Republic of Korea*, p. 42.

CHAPTER 4: AN INDEPENDENT SOUTH KOREA, A DIVIDED PENINSULA

7. Quoted in Oberdorfer, *The Two Koreas*, p. 34.

8. Oberdorfer, *The Two Koreas*, p. 36.

CHAPTER 5: THE ARTS IN KOREA

9. Steinberg, *The Republic of Korea*, p. 25.

10. *A Handbook of Korea*, p. 199.

11. Kyung Cho Chung et al., *The Korea Guidebook*, 5th ed. Boston: Houghton Mifflin, 1991, p. 75 .

12. *A Handbook of Korea*, p. 172.

13. *Faces: The Magazine About People.* Peterborough, NH: Cobblestone Publishing Company, April 1997, p. 27.

CHAPTER 6: AT HOME AND AT SCHOOL

14. Oberdorfer, *The Two Koreas*, p. 8.

15. Quoted in Michael Baker, "South Korea Ends a Taboo,

Strikes Blow for True Love," *Christian Science Monitor*, August 4, 1997, p. 6.

16. Elizabeth K. Lee, *The Koreans*. Seoul: Korean Overseas Information Service, 1989, p. 56.

17. Quoted in Baker, "South Korea Ends a Taboo, Strikes Blow for True Love," p. 6.

18. Steinberg, *The Republic of Korea*, p. 80.

CHAPTER 7:
THE ECONOMY AND SOUTH-NORTH RELATIONS

19. Quoted in Nicholas D. Kristof, "South Korea's New President Appeals to North to End Decades of Division," *New York Times*, February 25, 1998, p. A8.

20. Quoted in David Holley and Sonni Efron, "Despite Bailout, South Koreans Remain Upbeat," *Los Angeles Times*, December 7, 1997, p. 3.

21. Quoted in David Sanger, "Shaky Asia, New Shivers," *New York Times*, November 24, 1997, p. A1.

22. Quoted in Kristof, "South Korea's New President Appeals to North to End Decades of Division," p. A8.

23. Quoted in Annie Nakao, "Peace Talk Stirs Hope for Bay's Koreans," *San Francisco Examiner*, April 17, 1996, p. A1.

24. Quoted in Kristof, "South Korea's New President Appeals to North to End Decades of Division," p. A8.

25. *A Handbook of Korea*, p. 315.

26. Interview with the author, May 26, 1998.

27. Quoted in Holley and Efron, "Despite Bailout, South Koreans Remain Upbeat," p. 3.

28. Quoted in Holley and Efron, "Despite Bailout, South Koreans Remain Upbeat," p. 3.

CHRONOLOGY

B.C.

3000
Migratory peoples from Manchuria and Siberia settle on Korean peninsula, establish communities

2333
Koreans mark this year as the point at which their founder, Tan-gun, began his reign on Korean peninsula

A.D.

1st century
Various city-states established; northern part of peninsula conquered by Chinese

4th century
Three major kingdoms develop on peninsula; the Koguryo kingdom defeated the Chinese, and the kingdoms of Shilla and Paekche also emerge. Buddhism makes its way to the peninsula from China, as does Confucianism

668
Shilla joins with China to defeat Koguryo and Paekche; before end of century, Chinese are expelled from peninsula; kingdom of Shilla rules for 250 years

935
Shilla is overthrown by Koryo dynasty from Koguryo region

mid-12th century
Movable type is developed for book printing

13th century
Several Mongolian invasions; Mongols expelled by mid–fourteenth century

1392
General Yi Song-gye overthrows the Koryo dynasty and establishes the Yi dynasty, which will rule for five hundred

years; Confucianism becomes the court philosophy; Buddhism falls out of favor

1440s
King Sejong introduces the Korean alphabet, *han-gul*

1592
Toyotomi Hideyoshi from Japan attacks Korea, hoping to eventually conquer China. Hideyoshi is defeated by Korean Admiral Yi. Hideyoshi returns five years later, but dies during the siege, and his army retreats to Japan

17th century
The *yangban* class begins its decline; by end of century, Christian missionaries from China arrive in Korea

19th century
Christians are persecuted in first half of century. In the second half of the century, European countries and the United States force Korea into trade agreements; Japan also pushes for more trade relations, and forces Korea to sign treaties that are disadvantageous to Korea; it exerts more strength in manipulating Korean economy, and arranges for assassination of Queen Min

1894–1895
Japan soundly defeats China in Sino-Japanese War, allowing Japan to tighten its grip on Korea

1904–1905
Russia goes to war with Japan, and is defeated. In helping end the conflict, the United States acknowledges Japan's supremacy in Korea

1910
Korea is annexed to Japanese empire

1919
Japanese soldiers kill thousands of Koreans when they gather for huge demonstrations calling for Korean independence and publicly proclaim a Declaration of Independence

1945
Japan surrenders to the United States to end World War II. Korea is liberated, but occupied in north by Soviet Union and in south by United States

1948
The Republic of Korea is formed in the south, with Syngman Rhee as president. In the north, the Democratic People's Republic of Korea is established

1950
North Korea attacks the south on June 25, beginning the Korean War. Seoul is captured within three days

1953
Armistice to end combat is signed by North Korea, China, and United States on July 27

1960
Rhee is reelected president in corrupt elections; upon massive public demonstrations, he steps down in April and leaves Korea. In July a new national assembly and president are elected amid continued public unrest

1961
South Korean military stages coup, led by Park Chung Hee. He rewrites the constitution and restructures government, putting all branches of it under his control. He also does away with elections, but under pressure from United States reinstates them

1971
Park is almost defeated in presidential election; he declares martial law throughout South Korea

1979
Park is assassinated in October; amid efforts to reform constitution, another military leader, Chun Doo Hwan, takes control of government in December

May 1980
Student demonstrations demand lifting of martial law as well as presidential elections. Dissident and sometimes presidential candidate Kim Dae Jung is arrested on political charges; large protest gatherings in Kwangju, Kim's home region, end as military kills at least 240 citizens on May 27. The "Kwangju uprising" remains a sensitive political issue for many years. In the meantime, Kim Dae Jung is accused of and found guilty of planning the Kwangju demonstrations, and is sentenced to death

August 1980
Chun is "elected" president by the National Conference for Unification, which he established. He promised to serve no more than seven years as president

January 1981
Chun is invited to visit White House in Washington, D.C., to be received by President Ronald Reagan, as long as Kim Dae Jung's life is spared. Chun accepts the invitation and Kim is saved from execution

June 1987
Chun agrees to step down, but wants his handpicked successor, Roh Tae Woo, to be the next president. In the face of massive protests, Roh surprises the South Korean public by agreeing to run for president in a national election, scheduled for December 1987

December 1987
Roh Tae Woo is elected president when two other candidates split the opposition votes

September 1988
Seoul hosts Summer Olympic Games

1990
South Korea, now a major economic power, establishes full diplomatic relations with the Soviet Union, which forty-five years earlier caused the division of Korea; in 1992, South Korea establishes the same with China, which was North Korea's ally in the Korean War

1993
Kim Young Sam is elected president

1994
American and South Korean military secretly prepare for war against North Korea, which appears to be developing a nuclear bomb. In June, former U.S. president Jimmy Carter visits North Korea and helps defuse the situation

1997
Now an international economic powerhouse, South Korea begins to experience financial troubles: large companies receive international financial help only if they downsize

their companies; amid the turmoil, Kim Dae Jung is elected
president, on his fourth try for the office

1998
South Korea grapples with its financial difficulties (higher
rates of unemployment and bankruptcies); after a four-
year period of silence, south and north plan once more
the unification talks that have started and stopped many
times during the past twenty-five years, but North Korea
withdraws over issue of American troops on the peninsula

SUGGESTIONS FOR FURTHER READING

Facts About Korea. Seoul: Korean Overseas Information Service, 1993. Comprehensive information about South Korea; its history, people, and culture.

William H. Mathews, *South Korea in Pictures.* Minneapolis: Lerner, 1989. Describes the geography, history, government, people and economy of South Korea.

Patricia McMahon, *Chi-hoon: A Korean Girl.* Honesdale, PA: Caroline House, 1993. This book about eight-year-old Chi-hoon illustrates the daily life—school, family, and friends—in modern-day Seoul of one South Korean child.

Nami Rhee, *The Magic Spring: A Korean Folktale.* New York: G. P. Putnam's Sons, 1993. A traditional folktale of an old married couple who discover a fountain of youth, and what happens when their greedy neighbor finds out about it, too. The book is illustrated with watercolors painted on Korean rice paper, and characters from Korea's *han-gul* alphabet accompany the text.

Helen S. Kim, *The Long Season of Rain.* New York: Holt, 1995. A novel about a South Korean family whose life changes when an orphan boy comes to live with them.

On-Line Information:

Visit KoreaNet at **http://www.iworld.net:80/korea** to learn more about politics, history, culture, and travel in South Korea.

WORKS CONSULTED

Republic of Korea, APA Publications, 1989. Looks at the history, culture, and sites of interest in the Republic of Korea.

A Handbook of Korea. 9th ed. Seoul: Korean Overseas Information Service, 1993. Issued by the South Korean government, this book includes a comprehensive look at South Korea, including its history, government structure, geography, relations with North Korea, and various aspects of South Korean culture.

Kyung Cho Chung et al., *The Korea Guidebook*. 5th ed. Boston: Houghton Mifflin, 1991. Provides a guide to South Korean history and culture as well as information for those who visit.

Bruce Cumings, *Korea's Place in the Sun: A Modern History*. New York: W. W. Norton, 1997. The author writes of twentieth-century Korea's emergence as a major player in the world's economy.

Faces: The Magazine About People, April 1997. Peterborough, NH: Cobblestone Publishing Company. This monthly magazine for children looks at cultures and people around the world.

Russell Warren Howe, *The Koreans: Passion and Grace*. San Diego: Harcourt, Brace, Jovanovich, 1988. The author illustrates the influence of Korean thought and culture on everyday life in South Korea.

Elizabeth K. Lee, *The Koreans*. Seoul: Korean Overseas Information Service, 1989. Large, color photographs illustrate this book that describes the history and cultural traditions of the South Korean people.

Don Oberdorfer, *The Two Koreas: A Contemporary History*. Reading, MA: Addison-Wesley, 1997. This book concentrates on the last quarter-century of historical events in both South and North Korea.

David Steinberg, *The Republic of Korea: Economic Transformation and Social Change.* Boulder, CO: Westview Press, 1989. South Korea's history and culture are examined.

INDEX

PICTURE CREDITS

About the Author

Jean K. Williams has written several books for children. She studied journalism at Ohio State University, and has been a freelance writer for several years. She lives in Cincinnati, Ohio, with her husband, Brian, and their four children, Patricia, Suzanne, John, and Charlie.